Fresh Market
W·I·S·C·O·N·S·I·N

Recipes, Resources and Stories
Celebrating
Wisconsin Farm Markets
and Roadside Stands

*To Kathi & Dennis;
Happy marketing!
Terese Allen*

By Terese Allen

Cover design by Dunn & Associates Advertising Design
in Hayward, Wisconsin

Published by

AMHERST
PRESS

Fresh Market
W·I·S·C·O·N·S·I·N

First Edition.

Library of Congress Catalog Number 93-70423

ISBN 0-942495-26-8

A special thanks goes to The Farm Market in Wautoma for their help in staging our front cover shot.

Also by Terese Allen
The Ovens of Brittany Cookbook ISBN 0-942495-11-X

This book was printed on recycled paper by:

Amherst Press
A division of Palmer Publications, Inc.
P.O. Box 296
Amherst, WI 54406

TABLE OF CONTENTS

ACKNOWLEDGMENTS

After two growing seasons gathering material for this book at Wisconsin farmers' markets and roadside stands, I owe thanks to many people. First of all, a big thank you goes to all the market managers, vendors and customers who graciously shared their recipes, their knowledge of farming and direct marketing, their enthusiasm for fresh market food and the best ways to cook with it. No matter where I went, I almost always came away personally renewed by the good-naturedness and goodwill of the market people I met. I'd especially like to thank those vendors at the Wednesday and Saturday farmers' markets in Madison who regularly make me feel welcome at their stands. Some I don't even know by name, but all I count as friends.

I'm grateful to marketing specialist John Cottingham and former graduate student Jean Murphy of the University of Wisconsin-Platteville for their helpful research materials and their support of the project. There were others like them from all over the state—local librarians, historians, county extension agents and more—who assisted in many significant ways.

The recipes in this book went through multiple testings and thanks go to family members and friends who helped—especially the ones who kept coming back for more: my sisters Lutie Allen-Voreis and Judy Ullmer, and my nieces Claire Reinke, Ellen Klimek and Beth Zellner.

And then there's JB—Jim Block—the one who gets up at 5:45 on Saturday mornings (after Friday night softball) to come to the market with me. The one who no longer flinches when I suddenly yell "Stop!" on the highway—but calmly pulls over so we can visit yet another roadside stand. Life with JB is fun, full, challenging, rich, joyful. I'm thankful for him, grateful to him.

Finally, I'd like to express my respect for, and gratitude to, the small farmers and food producers of Wisconsin—the ones who really deserve most of the credit being assigned here. They work extremely hard and take tremendous risks to do what they do best: serve and nourish the rest of us. Without them, Wisconsin would simply not be . . . Wisconsin.

Terese Allen

This book is dedicated to my sisters:
Judy, Susie, Lutie, Jane, Mary and Judy Ann
and to my brothers:
Mark, Tom, John and Paul.

INTRODUCTION

" *W herever the market, there is a picture of Wisconsin's bounty and changing seasons. Spring brings trays of bedding plants, along with early rhubarb, asparagus and winter parsnips. Soon come the first strawberries, dainty peas and radishes tied up as pretty as red flowers. Summer rushes in with sweet corn, new potatoes, carrots, apples, cucumbers, beans and bundles of daisies, zinnias and glads. Autumn fairs are really harvest fairs with the rich golds of pumpkins and squash, pearly cauliflower, great spikes of Brussels sprouts and carrots by the truckload . . . you have an irresistible assortment.* "
Loren H. Osman, Wisconsin Trails magazine, May/June 1989

Welcome to the farmers' market! This book is a celebration of Wisconsin fresh market foods and the people who produce and sell them. It's a fond look at our seasonal markets—what they offer us, who is offering it, and how we can best take advantage of it all.

You'll find an up-to-date list of farmers' markets statewide, a harvest calendar and produce selection guide, storage and preparation hints and features on Wisconsin markets and roadside stands. You'll get to know growers, market managers and customers, and learn about the state's less familiar edibles—foods like ginseng and morel mushrooms.

You'll also find recipes. Inspired by the glorious vegetables, fruits and products of today's farm stands and markets, the recipes come from Wisconsin growers, market enthusiasts and my own kitchen. We highlight standard favorites like corn and tomatoes, as well as regional specialties like maple syrup, wild rice and cranberries. Fresh fruits and vegetables dominate—as they do at all seasonal markets—but anything that's sold at Wisconsin fresh food markets or roadside stands was considered fair game for this book: rainbow trout, free-range chickens, goat cheese, blackberry syrup, fresh herbs, hickory nuts, etc. We cover a lot of territory, but don't attempt to be comprehensive—that would take volumes.

This is not a collection of country recipes or ethnic dishes. Nor is it an attempt to break new culinary ground. The recipes are about what's cooking *today* in Wisconsin kitchens . . . city kitchens, country kitchens, family and gourmet kitchens, and above all, kitchens where fresh, from-scratch cooking is respected and enjoyed. We've tried to steer clear of flash-in-the-pan trends as well as overdone relics. Influenced by a range of culinary traditions and philosophies, we aimed for honest, easy-going preparations that make flavor and freshness a priority.

That kind of emphasis naturally—and happily—yields many healthful preparations. However, with the on-going barrage of new information about nutrition, pesticides and food additives, and with nearly every item on our tables branded a suspect, even the farmers' market can't offer a health guarantee. The thinking in this book is that if we're buying locally (and hopefully, organically), if we're cooking simply and eating seasonally, then we're probably making healthy choices.

Of course, we're talking about the Dairy State here. What's fresh and local—and very much "Wisconsin"—can also be what's high-fat and heavy on the cholesterol. In this book, we don't cut dairy out of the picture, but we do watch it—and we make it worth our while when we do indulge. Substitutions and other hints for healthy cooking are scattered throughout the book.

Your own substitutions are welcome—even encouraged—wherever there are ingredients you may be avoiding. Many products on the market today can help cut the fat in your life, products like cholesterol-free, reduced-calorie mayonnaise, yogurt, and low-fat cheeses. Some are good, some aren't. We leave those decisions up to you.

The first chapter is a look at farmers' markets in general, and at all the compelling reasons—culinary, economic, social, environmental, and health-related—for attending them. There's some historical background and a focus on Wisconsin as a prime farm market state.

The recipes are written with the average cook and the average kitchen in mind. If some recipes appear lengthy, it's because the intent was to err on the side of too much information instead of too little. Most are simple and straightforward. Again, feel free to experiment with substitutions to fit your health needs or culinary fancy.

Please note that flour refers to the unbleached, all-purpose type; eggs are Grade A large; and when a recipe calls for milk, skim, 1%, 2% or whole milk may be selected.

Whether you're a die-hard market fan, a fair-weather friend or a newcomer, the aim of this book is to get you out there—to the market, to soak in the fresh air and friendliness, to get to know real food, and to make the purchases that support our communities, protect our earth and bring us so much pleasure.

Terese Allen
Madison, Wisconsin

Fresh Market
W·I·S·C·O·N·S·I·N

TO MARKET, TO MARKET

TO MARKET, TO MARKET

"*I*t *was a feast for all the senses, not just the palate.*"
Perla Meyers, "From Market to Kitchen Cookbook," 1979

"Part theater, part street fair and a produce shopper's dream—farmers' markets are springing up everywhere, revitalizing city neighborhoods, bringing shoppers and farmers together, inspiring local chefs and bringing you the freshest, ripest, most delicious fruits and vegetables." Glamour magazine, July 1991

There are as many good reasons to go to farm markets as there are ears in a cornfield. Good food, of course, tops the list. Study after study shows that quality is the number one reason people pause at roadside stands or get up early on Saturday to get to the market. They do it because they know that's where they'll find just-picked freshness, full-flavored ripeness and lush variety. "Reliance on out-of-season foods makes the gastronomic year an endlessly boring repetition," said British/American journalist Roy Andries De Groot, but at the market, "the right food always comes at the right time."

For all of us concerned about our health and the health of the earth—and thank goodness those numbers are growing greater—the availability of organic produce at open markets is a big plus. Agricultural pollution is a part of the environmental crisis we face today, and is central to an entire array of food safety issues. Wholesome food—that is, food grown without the use of chemical fertilizers, herbicides, insecticides and fungicides—helps sustain both the people who eat it and the land it grows on. Furthermore, buying locally and seasonally saves fuel and resources wasted on long-distance transportation, reduces throw-away packaging and encourages crop diversity.

For the health-conscious, cutting down on fats and eating more fiber comes easy when shopping is done where fresh fruits and vegetables dominate. Seasonal markets are especially welcome in Wisconsin, where we have, by necessity, a get-it-while-you-can-attitude about fresh produce. Many Midwesterners continue to can, freeze or dry their market purchases not just for the economy of it, but to prolong flavor and nutrition. Nothing brightens a cold Wisconsin winter like the healthy taste of summer captured in a jar.

But the allure of seasonal markets goes beyond good taste, beyond even health and environmental concerns. Farmers' markets are important in a society where people are increasingly alienated from one another. "Walking along the earthy lanes and seeing the seasons reflected in all the displays seems to turn back time and remind us of our close, comforting connections with people and with the natural order of the universe," said cookbook author Marion Cunningham in California Magazine (June 1988). She knows we are hungry for more than food. "In addition to the produce, we are nourished by our sense of communication, that communal sense of life and beauty and being outdoors with other people."

The late food-great James Beard put it another way: "I love the alive, throbbing excitement of the market, the busy movement of the shoppers, the common denominator of food that brings people together."

Most of us love the market hustle and bustle, but for some it can be a hassle. Grocery stores may be more convenient and more weather-proof than the weekly farmers' market. Shoppers must beware of buy-and-sell stands that may be making false claims about product origin and freshness. But when we shop locally, direct from the source, we can better educate ourselves about what we're consuming.

Only at farm markets do we come face to face with the people who grow our food. We can ask questions, get to know each other, learn to trust each other. At the local produce stand, shoppers experience a personalized attention unheard of in supermarkets. Vendors can offer advice or make changes based on their real knowledge of the needs, tastes and concerns of their customers. Problems are handled quickly and directly—or better yet, are avoided altogether. That's not to say it's a perfect relationship. What's important, though, is that at the farmers' market, there *is* a relationship.

People issues are a fact of life at green markets. Market managers and growers deal with sticky subjects like stall assignments, price wars and disgruntled grocers jealous of the competition. Farmers' markets thrive and prosper because of their diversity, but occasionally discrimination must be overcome if newer vendors—like the Hmong immigrants in Wisconsin —are resented instead of welcomed.

One complaint at larger farmers' markets is that products and prices have gotten "yuppified." Baby vegetables and exotic cheeses attract a wealthier, trendier clientele—and that's good for business. What really fuels Wisconsin markets, however, is the demand for plain food at plain prices. The growing popularity of farm markets nationwide "is not simply about people who want to pay dearly for a perfectly dear tomato," says Hilary Baum of Public Market Partners (quoted in the New York Times, August 21, 1991). "Markets continue to thrive . . . by offering bargains for bulk buying of in-season produce."

The buyer isn't the only one who can get a good deal at farm markets. Growers who sell direct can earn up to three times the amount they would selling wholesale. Unhampered by the limitations of shippers, farmers can also grow a greater variety of produce, which reduces the chance of disease destroying an entire season's crop and allows greater flexibility in responding to market changes. To small farmers facing today's economic squeeze, direct marketing can mean the difference between success and foreclosure.

"Ultimately it comes down to realizing the necessity of the land . . . and our connection to it," says Alice Waters in an essay called "The Farm-Restaurant Connection." "As restaurateurs and ordinary consumers meet the people who grow their food, they acquire an interest in the future of farms, of rural communities, and of the environment . . . Fresh, locally grown, seasonal foodstuffs are more than an attractive fashion or a quaint, romantic notion: They are a fundamental part of a sustainable economy and agriculture."

Economic benefits extend to cities and towns, also. There's a reason the Chamber of Commerce supports its local farmers' market . . . the crowd it draws means business, and that means a stimulated local economy. In Milwaukee, for example, the Department of City Development opened three "Green Markets" specifically to utilize city-owned open spaces and help resuscitate neighborhoods. "It's a win-win situation," says Cecelia Gilbert, the exuberant manager of the city's flourishing markets. "It's good for farmers, good for consumers, good for the city."

A Fitting Survival

"Farm markets have been with us since the beginning of time, when those from the country walked, rode horseback or filled their wagons with the produce they had grown to bring it to a gathering place to sell and exchange wares. One of the earliest to do this was Lydia, the seller of purple, the dye which was so important in Biblical times."

Peg Park, West Allis Star, date unknown

Open markets characterized humankind's earliest organization into community. The growth of markets signaled the growth of civilization. During our own colonial days, fairs operated in nearly every town and were politically regulated from very early on. In Wisconsin, fur traders and European settlers bartered with native peoples. The recording of established markets in our state began in the mid-1800s.

Two of the oldest continuous regular markets in the state take place in Watertown and Princeton. Watertown's first market was held October 6, 1860, and the Princeton Cattle Fair, still faithfully held on the first Wednesday of each month, emerged from early county fairs beginning in 1856. According to "Wisconsin Then and Now," a publication of the State Historical Society, Stevens Point's market dates from 1870 and was a feature of the Public Square—also known as Polish Square, since most of the farmers who brought their livestock and produce to sell were Polish immigrants.

The public market, however, "was doomed by a changing society," observed geographer Jane Pyle in her analysis of farmers' markets in The Geographical Review (1971). The growth of cities, new food preservation techniques, agricultural improvements and major changes in transportation all led to the inevitable decline of direct marketing. By the early 20th century, wrote Pyle, "the retail functions of city markets were often replaced by wholesalers in central locations and by neighborhood grocers."

Despite this, farmers' markets held their own. A 1918 Census Bureau study showed that while the process of decline continued, markets offering fresh produce directly to the consumer were still in demand, especially during hard times. Green Bay's market is a good example of this—it opened in 1917 with public promises to reduce food costs, and it saw quick success.

Even—maybe especially—in today's wound-up world of colossal foodstores and microwave dinners, the outdoor markets survive. "Over the years," noted Pyle, "the market has been stoutly defended by those who see in it old-fashioned virtues of individuality and direct connection with Mother Earth, has been attacked by those who see in it an unwarranted subsidy of inefficiency . . . and is faithfully patronized by those who prefer the quality of freshness over quantity, or even over price."

Pyle concluded her study with a prediction. She cited several markets which gave "evidence of success that may herald another upswing in the fortune of the farmers' market."

She was right on the money. Farmers' markets haven't just survived since Pyle did her research in 1971—they've thrived. Public Market Partners, a group that assists urban markets, estimates that more than 2,000 new markets have opened across the country between the mid-70s and early 90s. Roadside stands also increased by the thousands.

We're realizing just how hungry we are—hungry for fresh, satisfying food. Thirsty for a sense of community. Craving a healthier environment and a fair shake for small farmers. Born of necessity, fed by demand, direct marketing is going strong—growing, you might say, like zucchini in August.

On Wisconsin

"People say the food just tastes better from our stands."
   Marketing Specialist John Cottingham, University of Wisconsin-Extension, Platteville

The Badger State is at the forefront of today's market movement. With over 90 regular farmers' markets and countless roadside stands and pick-your-own operations, Wisconsin joins agricultural giants like California and Pennsylvania as one of the most "market-ed" states in the nation.

The Dane County Farmers' Market in Madison is probably the largest in the Midwest. The variety is dizzying—over 150 vendors over the course of a season—and the crowds are enormous—up to twenty thousand shoppers gather on Saturdays from late April to early November. It doesn't take a crowd, however, to make a market: small towns like Frederic and Richland Center have flourishing markets with as few as five or ten vendors. Most typical are markets that see 25-50 vendors during peak season.

In Wisconsin, no two farmers' markets are the same. The one at Tuckwood House, a crafts-and-antique shop in Fennimore, is privately operated. Owner Dixie Miles sponsors the weekly event to draw business to her store. "Nobody comes to just buy vegetables and walk away," says Dixie with a smile in her voice. Dixie's business-booster doubles as an asset to the Fennimore community. "The older people really love it," she notes.

More often than not, a local business organization or the Chamber of Commerce takes the lead in organizing and promoting a town market. West Bend's Downtown Marketplace Association manages their Saturday market and handles its advertising and promotions. On their annual "Dairy Day," marketers can eat at a "calf-eteria," listen to country "moosic" or enjoy the Celebrity Cow Milking Contest.

The state's Department of Development sponsors "Wisconsin Main Street," a program that helps over two dozen communities organize and promote downtown revitalization. Farmers' markets are part of the strategy—and part of the success story—in Main Street towns like Viroqua and Eau Claire.

Sometimes the public market is handled by city or county officials. In Green Bay, the City Sealer (the person who regulates weights and measures in city commerce) has traditionally held the position of market manager.

Madison's market is run by a non-profit corporation, Westfield's by a growers' cooperative. The Department of Agriculture, the University of Wisconsin-Extension, the Farm Bureau and other farm-support organizations often lend a hand in getting and keeping a market going.

"Farmers' markets are as diverse as the people who produce for them," concluded University of Wisconsin-Extension market specialist John Cottingham in a 1992 statewide farmers' market study, co-authored by graduate student Jean Murphy. John's own advice—"let the market make the rules"—is generally followed when it comes to regulations, which vary as widely as the management structures do. Markets must answer these questions, and more: Crafts or no crafts? Buy-and-sell or vendor-grown goods only? Prepared foods or just produce? What about cheese, meats and fish? The answers change from market to market.

There are roadside stands with homegrown zucchini and cucumbers and signs like this one: "Self Service. Put Money In Box. God and You Know Who Pay." There are slick, gourmet farm markets that house delis, bakeries and gift shops, and sponsor giant harvest festivals. Fresh, local produce is the drawing card of every Wisconsin market, but each one provides its own special flavors to enliven your visit and make your meal.

Most of Wisconsin's farm stands and markets are concentrated where the greatest number of farms—and people—are located: in the southern half of the state, and especially to the east, around Milwaukee. Even in chilly northern towns like Hurley and Rice Lake, however, the farmers gather or set up a lone stand, and the customers respond.

Small or large, old or new, on Main Street, at the end of a driveway, or in the Pamida parking lot on the edge of town, fresh food markets dot the state's landscape. From Algoma to Wausau, from Bayfield to Beloit, you're never far from a taste of Wisconsin.

Just Right

"Food that tastes good, and is good for you is not just a private indulgence but a force for sustaining families and communities, the end result of larger goods that benefit everyone . . . [We gain] a sense of the thread that runs from a glass of wine or a simmering pot to family meals to markets to farms, and thence to the past traditions and future life of all our kind and of the earth itself."

Robert Clark, editor, "Our Sustainable Table," 1990

Farmers' markets aren't just about our food. They're about our health, our history, our environment. They're about having fun. They tell us stories about ourselves and teach us what the TV can't. They bring us together.

There's something *right* about going to the market. We may not be able to grow or hunt our food, but we can *know* it, and we can know the people who do grow it. It's a profound connection.

So, go on. Get to the market. It'll make you feel just right.

Fresh Market
W·I·S·C·O·N·S·I·N

SPRING VEGETABLES

Wilted Watercress (Mom's Recipe)
4 servings

Watercress has a peppery tang that matches well with the sweet-sour flavor of a hot bacon dressing. This is a three-generation recipe from Bill Warner, a Dane County Farmers' Market vendor who's known for plump, beautiful produce and for getting it out early in the season. He got this Wilted Watercress recipe from his mother, Rachel Jordan of Dodgeville, who inherited it from her mother.

Note: To add an extra touch of Wisconsin, substitute maple syrup or honey for the sugar.

1 very large or two medium bunches fresh watercress
¼ pound bacon
¾ cup sliced onion
3 tablespoons vinegar
1 tablespoon sugar
1 teaspoon prepared horseradish or mustard (optional)
Salt and freshly ground black pepper

1. Clean watercress in cold water and drain. Dry in salad spinner or clean towel. Place in large bowl and set aside.
2. Chop bacon and cook over medium heat until crispy. Remove bacon with slotted spoon, drain on paper towels and reserve.
3. Pour off all but ¼ cup of the drippings in the pan. Add onions and cook over medium heat until wilted. Add vinegar, sugar, optional horseradish or mustard, and 1-2 tablespoons water. Stir until sugar is dissolved. Add reserved bacon bits and heat through. Season with salt and pepper to taste.
4. Pour over watercress; toss until just wilted. Serve immediately.

Bill Warner/Rachel Jordan
Nature's Acres
Dodgeville, Wisconsin

"The market just makes you itch to buy and to cook."

James Beard

BASICS IN BRIEF: CROUTONS

Cut leftover bread into small cubes. Melt butter or heat olive oil in a small pan; add dried herbs and/or minced garlic and cook gently for a minute or two. Toss croutons with butter or oil mixture and bake in preheated 400-degree oven 8-12 minutes, until toasted. Cool thoroughly and store airtight.

Charlemagne Salad with Hot Brie Dressing
6 servings

Fresh lettuce and garlic croutons are dressed with a warm, creamy Brie-based sauce. This is an elegant and luscious way to feature spring greens, and makes an excellent first course to a special dinner.

Recipe contributor Susan Smith of Blue Valley Gardens suggests the following greens for this salad: Romance (romaine), Winter Density, Boston Burgundy or Melody (spinach). You could use all of one variety, but why resist the assortment of tastes and textures that's available at spring produce stands? A mixture of two or more greens will give the salad character.

Note: Although the Brie rind is edible, it's not used in this recipe. You can chop the reserved rind and add it to salads or quiche, or simply nibble it with crackers.

8 ounces ripe Brie, chilled
2 medium or 3 small heads romaine or leaf lettuce, OR 1
  pound spinach, stems removed
1½ cups garlic croutons (See side bar)
⅓ cup olive oil
4 teaspoons minced shallots or green onions
2 teaspoons minced garlic
½ cup white wine vinegar
2 tablespoons fresh lemon juice
3 teaspoons Dijon-style mustard
Freshly ground black pepper

1. Remove rind from chilled Brie with a sharp knife; reserve rind for another use. Cut cheese into small pieces and allow to come to room temperature.
2. Wash greens in cold water. Tear into bite-sized pieces; dry in salad spinner or clean towels. Toss with croutons in a very large bowl.
3. Warm oil in a heavy skillet. Add shallots or green onions and garlic; cook over low heat until golden, about 3 minutes. Stir in vinegar, lemon juice, mustard and several grindings of pepper.
4. Add the cheese a little at a time, stirring constantly.
5. When all the cheese is melted, toss hot dressing with greens and croutons. Serve immediately, and pass the pepper mill. (Note: The dressing may be held and gently reheated just before serving.)

Susan and Matthew Smith
Blue Valley Gardens
Blue Mounds, Wisconsin

Spinach Pie with Feta Cheese and Fresh Dill
6 servings

Spinach, feta and dill are a well-known and delicious combination; the flavors really come alive in this pie only if you use fresh, young spinach leaves and chopped fresh dill. It's just not worth it otherwise.

1 tablespoon olive oil
½ cup minced onion
8-12 ounces fresh spinach, stems removed, cleaned and coarsely chopped
6 ounces feta cheese, broken into small chunks
3 eggs
1 cup milk
2 tablespoons chopped fresh dill
¼ teaspoon salt
½ teaspoon black pepper
¼ cup freshly grated Parmesan cheese
1 9-inch deep dish pie crust, unbaked (see side bar)
3-4 tomato slices, halved OR 16-20 black olives, halved (optional)

1. Preheat oven to 350 degrees. Heat oil in large skillet; add onion and cook over medium-low heat until translucent.
2. Raise heat to high and add spinach. Toss and cook until all the spinach is wilted and some of the liquid has evaporated, 4-5 minutes. Turn off heat, let cool 5 minutes. Sprinkle feta over spinach.
3. Whisk eggs, milk, dill, salt and pepper in large bowl. Sprinkle Parmesan cheese onto bottom of pie crust.
4. Stir spinach and feta into egg mixture. Gently pour into crust. For an optional garnish, arrange tomatoes or olive halves around outer rim of pie, pressing them very lightly into the surface without submerging them. Bake 40-50 minutes, until center is just set. Do not overbake. Let pie cool 10-15 minutes before serving.

BASICS IN BRIEF: PIE CRUST

For 1 double or two single deep-dish pies.

2½ cups flour
1 tablespoon sugar (optional)
1 teaspoon salt
6 tablespoons cold shortening, cut into small pieces
5 tablespoons cold butter, cut into small pieces
8-10 tablespoons ice water

Mix flour, optional sugar and salt by hand or in food processor. Cut in shortening and butter until they are the size of sunflower seeds. (If you're using a food processor for this, use the pulse button and be careful not to overmix, then transfer mixture to a bowl.) Sprinkle in ice water, one tablespoon at a time, while you toss mixture lightly with a fork. Stop adding water when mixture holds together in small lumps. Turn dough onto a double layer of plastic wrap. Gather wrap very tightly around dough to form a ball. Chill two or more hours.

To roll out crust: Handle dough as little as possible during this process. Unwrap dough and place on a floured work surface, then divide it in half. (Freeze one half for the future if you're not using it now.) Press down on dough with your hand to form a disk.

Gently roll out dough with an even motion to form a circle. Sprinkle on more flour if crust gets sticky.

Loosen crust from work surface with a thin, flat utensil. To transfer crust to pie pan, fold it in quarters and unfold it once it's in the pan. Crimp the edges, patching any skimpy areas with excess dough.

If the recipe calls for a prebaked crust, prick it all over with a fork and chill until ready to pre-bake. Preheat oven to 400 degrees. Line crust with aluminum foil and fill it with dried beans to weight it. Bake 8 minutes, remove beans and foil, and continue to bake until crust is dry and golden brown, about 7-10 minutes. Cool and proceed with recipe.

SAVE THE SPINACH

Fresh spinach quickly loses flavor and nutrition when it gets water-logged, but the only way to get rid of its grit is to immerse the leaves in two or more changes of cold water. So work quickly, and if the spinach will be eaten raw, use a salad spinner or cotton towels to dry the tender leaves.

Spring Spinach Salad with Honey Onion Dressing
4 servings

Crunchy radishes, sharp green onions and young carrots make this spinach salad stand up and say "Spring." Other early season possibilities that could be added include mushrooms, snowpeas, watercress, asparagus and bok choy.

10-12 ounces fresh young spinach leaves, stems removed
½ cup toasted walnut or pecan halves (see page 149 for method)
1 cup grated carrots
½ cup sliced radishes
¼ cup chopped green onion
⅓ - ½ cup Honey Onion Dressing (page 147)
Freshly ground black pepper
4 hard-cooked eggs, quartered

Clean spinach in cold water; dry in salad spinner or clean towels. Combine with nuts and vegetables in large bowl. Toss with dressing and freshly ground black pepper to taste. Garnish with eggs.

Luna Circle Watercress Salad
2 servings

Luna Circle Farm, owned and operated by Tricia Bross and Ayla Heartsong of Gays Mills, is a small but successful organic operation that sells nearly all of its produce at two markets, one in Madison and one in La Crosse. Their watercress is wild-gathered and therefore not officially organic, although "it's picked from a clear spring at the base of a hill," says Ayla.

You'll need a young, mild watercress for this simple, honey-sweetened salad; taste the cress before you purchase it to make sure it's not too "hot" for you.

3-4 cups watercress (or use half watercress and half spinach)
⅔ cup grated carrot
2 hard-cooked eggs, diced
¼ cup mayonnaise or plain, no-fat yogurt
2 teaspoons honey
Salt and freshly ground black pepper to taste

Cut off root ends of watercress (and if using spinach, remove the stems). Wash gently in cold water, then dry in clean towel or salad spinner. Place in bowl and sprinkle with grated carrots and chopped eggs. Blend remaining ingredients and toss lightly with the salad. Serve immediately.

Tricia Bross
Luna Circle Farm
Gays Mills, Wisconsin

Shredded Chicken Sesame in Lettuce Cups
8-10 appetizer servings, 4 as a main course salad

Jeff Smith's "The Frugal Gourmet Cooks Three Ancient Cuisines" contains a recipe for an oriental chicken salad that triggered the idea for this Shredded Chicken Sesame in Lettuce Cups. There's a few changes from "the Frug's" recipe: lots of green onion plus a touch of hot pepper oil give the chicken salad a kick, and toasted sunflower seeds add a nutty crunch. Bright garnishes add color and flavor, and instead of bread or crackers, lettuce leaves are used as a fresh and healthy foil for the salad.

MARKETING FOR HEALTH

What should Americans eat to stay healthy? There's help with the answer to that controversial question with seven dietary guidelines recommended by the Department of Health and Social Services. A glance at the guidelines (plus one that's not on the official list) shows just how much shopping at farm markets and roadside stands can help us eat healthy.

Recommendation: Eat a variety of foods.

As the seasons and produce change, getting a variety of foods via the farmers' market—especially healthy fruits and vegetables—is simple and natural.

Recommendation: Maintain healthy weight.

The nutritious, low-fat foods that dominate the fresh market scene make calorie-conscious shopping easier. Leave the fatty snacks and sodas at the grocery store.

Recommendation: Choose a diet low in fat, saturated fat and cholesterol.

Most of what's available at the market is naturally low in fats and cholesterol—you can't go wrong.

Recommendation: Choose a diet with plenty of vegetables, fruits and grains.

This is what the farmers' market is all about!

Recommendation: Use sugars in moderation.

Some markets sell pastries and other prepared goods, but the abundant fresh produce makes it easy to make good choices.

Recommendation: Use salt in moderation.

You won't find rows of salty, high fat snacks at seasonal markets. The dishes you do prepare with market products will require less salt because they're made with fresh, more flavorful ingredients.

Recommendation: If you drink alcoholic beverages, do so in moderation.

The farmers' market is a great place to meet people, so you can skip the bars. And, there's no cover charge, no alcohol, just plenty of good food and great entertainment.

Recommendation: Avoid over-processed, over-preserved and pesticide-laden foods.

Add this one to the official list—and remember: there's nowhere better to shop for organically raised, natural foods than an outdoor market.

A nice way to present this is to mound the chicken salad on a large platter or individual plates, then surround with the fresh lettuce leaves and garnishes. Use a butterhead-type lettuce like Bibb or Buttercrunch; the small heads yield lettuce cups that are just the right size to fill with chicken for a hands-on appetizer or main course salad.

1 whole chicken, 2-3 pounds

Salad Dressing:

3 tablespoons tahini (sesame seed paste) or peanut butter
2 tablespoons dry sherry
2 tablespoons soy sauce
1 tablespoon dark sesame oil
1 tablespoon cider vinegar
1½ teaspoons minced garlic
1 teaspoon sugar
1 teaspoon finely grated fresh ginger root
½ teaspoon hot pepper oil or red pepper flakes
½ cup chopped green onion
Freshly ground black pepper to taste

Other Ingredients:

2 medium heads lettuce: Boston, Bibb or Buttercrunch
⅓ cup toasted sunflower seeds
Tomato wedges
Lemon wedges
Additional chopped green onion

1. Bring a large pot of water to boil; add chicken and simmer very gently 40 minutes. Drain, cool, and de-bone chicken. Shred the meat with a fork and place in a bowl.
2. Mix all dressing ingredients and toss with the chicken. Refrigerate until ready to serve.
3. Break lettuce leaves from the base of each head; rinse and pat dry. (Hold the lettuce leaves in a dry towel in the refrigerator until ready to serve.)
4. To serve: Fold sunflower seeds into the chicken. Portion lettuce leaves and chicken salad on individual plates or one large platter. Garnish with tomatoes, lemon wedges and additional green onion. Squeeze some of the lemon juice over all. Fill lettuce leaves with chicken salad and roll up to eat with your fingers.

Basmati Rice, Ham and Asparagus Salad
6-8 servings

This is one of the first recipes I want to make when asparagus hits the market stands. Basmati is a sweet, nutty-flavored rice that fills the room with a fabulous aroma when it cooks. Another special ingredient in this salad is balsamic vinegar, an intense red wine vinegar aged in oak barrels. Regular white or brown rice and any wine vinegar may be substituted for these ingredients and you'll still get excellent results.

4 tablespoons balsamic or red wine vinegar
2 garlic cloves, slightly crushed
2 tablespoons chopped fresh thyme OR 2 teaspoons dried thyme
Freshly ground black pepper
½ cup olive oil
1 ½ cups basmati, brown or converted white rice
1 teaspoon salt
½ pound asparagus: tough ends removed, chopped, blanched briefly and drained (See page 21 for blanching method)
½ pound lean ham, diced
⅓ cup chopped green onions

1. To make dressing: Combine vinegar, garlic cloves, thyme and several grindings of black pepper. Whisk in olive oil in a thin stream. Let stand 1-2 hours or more. Remove garlic.
2. Cook rice according to package instructions and let cool to room temperature.
3. To mix salad: Toss rice, dressing and remaining ingredients in a bowl. Season to taste with additional black pepper. Serve at room temperature.

ASPARAGUS TIPS

Asparagus is spring's succulent specialty. Look for spears with tight-budded tips at your local farmers' market, and don't worry about thick or thin for they are both delicious. Snap or cut off the tough ends and peel the stems with a potato peeler; you'll get maximum tenderness that way.

Above all, don't overcook asparagus! Bring an inch or two of water to boil in a stainless steel frying pan and drop the thickest spears in first. Don't cover the pan, or the aparagus will lose its bright greenness. When all the asparagus have been added and the water has simmered 1-3 minutes, lift a couple of spears out of the water with a fork. If they droop just a little, they are done. Thicker asparagus will take longer. Drain and serve hot (with butter or lemon juice); or rinse with cold water, pat the asparagus dry and serve room temperature or chilled (with olive oil and vinegar, herbed dressing or dips).

BASICS IN BRIEF: BLANCHING

Blanching is a method used to partially cook vegetables. Fresh vegetables are cooked briefly (1-2 minutes, more if they are very thick) in a large amount of rapidly boiling water in an uncovered pot. Keep the flame high and don't crowd the pot. Time it from the moment the water begins to bubble again. The vegetables are then cooled quickly—to stop the cooking—by running them under cold water or immersing them in ice water.

The blanching method is used when freezing garden produce like beans or asparagus, or to get tender but firm vegetables for salads and dip platters. Blanching is also a smart idea when you want to avoid overcooking vegetables, for the partially-cooked vegetables can be held at room temperature or chilled, then quickly sautéed with herbs or other flavorings at the very last minute.

The bright, intense color that results when vegetables are blanched adds an attractive touch, and the brief pre-cooking softens the hard crunch of raw vegetables without sacrificing crispness or tenderness. Vegetables that take well to blanching include broccoli, carrots, green beans, wax beans, asparagus and cauliflower.

Barely Dressed Asparagus Spears
3-4 servings

Easy to make, low in fat, intensely flavored, and handsome on the plate. To increase this recipe, double the amount of asparagus but use the same amount of dressing. You can also substitute broccoli, carrots, snow peas or other vegetables for the asparagus.

1 pound asparagus, tough ends removed
1 teaspoon minced garlic, mashed to a paste
2 tablespoons soy sauce
1 tablespoon dark sesame oil
1 teaspoon honey
Toasted sesame seeds (see page 149 for method)

1. Rolling each spear as you cut it, chop asparagus into attractive, diagonally cut 2-inch pieces. Blanch asparagus (see side bar, this page); it should retain some crunch and a bright green color. Cool quickly under running water or in ice water. Drain well and pat dry.

2. Combine garlic, soy sauce, sesame oil and honey in a medium bowl. Toss in the asparagus and let marinate in or out of the refrigerator at least two hours, stirring often. Sprinkle with toasted sesame seeds just before serving.

Asparagus Parmesan
3-4 servings

Colorful and delicious.

1 pound asparagus, tough ends removed
1 tablespoon butter (cut into bits) or olive oil
1 medium tomato, seeded and chopped
Salt and freshly ground black pepper
¼ cup freshly grated Parmesan cheese

1. Bring a pan of water to boil. Peel asparagus spears and add to pan. Blanch 2-3 minutes until barely tender. Rinse in cold water and drain.
2. Lightly grease a baking dish and place asparagus in it. Dot with butter or drizzle with olive oil. Sprinkle with chopped tomato. Season with salt and pepper to taste.
3. To cook: heat oven to 350 degrees. Bake asparagus 15 minutes, then sprinkle on Parmesan and bake 5 more minutes, until cheese is melted. Serve hot.

STAND BY YOUR ASPARAGUS

Take advantage of asparagus season and buy enough for several meals. You can keep asparagus fresh for several days by standing the spears upright in water and keeping them in the refrigerator. (Clip off the ends first, just like you would for flowers.)

Lemon Mayonnaise *(For Dipping Vegetables)*
Makes about 1 ½ cups

You won't believe how good fresh mayonnaise is until you try it. This easy Lemon Mayonnaise has a sunny flavor and a creamy yellow shade that complement chilled asparagus spears perfectly. Or try it with a platter of fresh or blanched dipping vegetables from the spring market stands: sugar snap peas, julienned kohlrabi, baby zucchini, radishes and slender scallions. (For blanching instructions, see page 21.)

This recipe takes only minutes, and you'll experience the rich satisfaction of a hollandaise sauce without all its cholesterol. The lemon zest is essential; use the section of your grater with the tiniest holes and grate only the bright yellow outer layer of the lemon. Grate the lemon *before* you juice it.

Leftover mayonnaise can be folded into chicken or tuna salad or spread on a sandwich.

1 lemon (for grated zest and 4 teaspoons lemon juice)
1 large egg or 2 egg whites
1 tablespoon cider or white wine vinegar
1 tablespoon Dijon-style mustard
¾ cup olive oil
½ cup canola or vegetable oil
1 teaspoon dried thyme
Salt and ground white pepper to taste

1. Finely grate outer layer of lemon. Juice enough of the lemon to get 4 teaspoons juice.
2. Blend egg (or egg whites), vinegar, lemon juice and mustard in a food processor or blender one minute. With the machine running, gradually add the oils in a very thin, steady stream through the opening in the lid of the machine. Add the thyme and lemon zest, plus salt and pepper to taste; process a few seconds longer. Refrigerate until ready to use.

Asparagus Strudel
8-10 servings

Here's a tempting, slightly corrupt way to prepare fresh asparagus. Buttery phyllo dough wraps around a filling of chopped asparagus, Swiss cheese, leeks and fresh dill.

1 pound peeled and chopped asparagus
Up to 8 tablespoons butter, divided
1 cup chopped leeks
8 ounces shredded Swiss cheese
2 eggs
2 tablespoons fresh lemon juice
2 tablespoons chopped fresh dill
⅛ teaspoon red cayenne pepper
1 teaspoon salt
¼ teaspoon ground black pepper
12 leaves phyllo dough (about ½ pound), thawed in refrigerator 24 hours, then brought to room temperature

1. Blanch asparagus; rinse and drain well (see side bar, page 21).
2. Melt 1 tablespoon butter in a skillet; add leeks and cook over medium heat until tender. Cool.

(continued on next page)

"I stick to asparagus which seems to inspire gentle thought."

Charles Lamb,
English writer

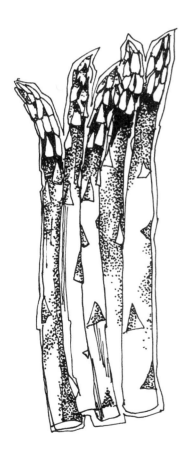

Asparagus Strudel *(continued)*

3. Mix aspargus, leeks, grated cheese, eggs, lemon juice, dill and seasonings in a large bowl. Preheat oven to 350 degrees.
4. Melt remaining butter. Layer 6 phyllo leaves on a work surface, lightly brushing butter on each layer (emphasize the outer edges). Place half the filling on short end and roll up tightly. Place seam side down on baking sheet. Repeat process with remaining dough and filling. Lightly brush both strudels with butter. Slash the top of each roll in several places to mark the serving sizes. Bake 30-40 minutes until golden brown. Slice and serve.

Susan and Matthew Smith
Blue Valley Gardens
Blue Mounds, Wisconsin

Puree of Asparagus Soup with Fresh Dill
3-4 servings

Tastes especially warm and good for lunch after a chilly spring morning at the market.

2 teaspoons butter or margarine
¾ cup chopped green onions, divided
1 pound asparagus, tough ends removed
3½ cups homemade chicken stock (recipe on page 54)
  or canned chicken broth
½ teaspoon dried dill seed
2 teaspoons chopped fresh dill
¼ teaspoon white pepper
Salt
2 tablespoons half-and-half (optional)

Garnishes:

Freshly grated Parmesan cheese
Additional chopped fresh dill

1. Melt butter or margarine in a medium saucepan. Add ½ cup green onions, cover and cook over low heat until wilted, about 5 minutes.
2. Chop asparagus. Reserve ½ of the tips for later use. Add asparagus, stock and dill seed to onions. Simmer 12-15 minutes, until asparagus is very tender.
3. Drain most of the liquid from the pot into a bowl. Puree

"Every Saturday morning, the two of us would set out with a warning from my mother not to buy too much. I can still remember my father winking at me and the sense of excitement we shared in discovering an unusual fruit, a new cheese or pastry. He always reminded me that markets were special, and so were the people who cared about food. He had a wonderful relationship with many of the local shopkeepers, who were always on the lookout for us, waiting to greet us warmly and urging us to sample cheeses, sausages or fruit. They were generous and full of good humor, and we were eager to chat and taste their delicious morsels . . . By the time we came home, we unpacked an assortment of foods that never really made much sense, but would often force my father into the kitchen to come up with a spur of the moment preparation . . .
Many of the best meals at our house were those impromptu ones."

Perla Meyers,
"From Market to Kitchen Cookbook," 1979

SCENES FROM THE MARKET: Milwaukee

Three-piece suits mix with overalls at Milwaukee's downtown market on a hot and sunny Wednesday. The city's work force is on lunch break, so business at the market is brisk. There's still time for some friendly bantering, however.

"I love to be outside," says a market supervisor. "I love to learn things from the farmers. I'm from Detroit. I thought food grew in cans." Laughter erupts.

The speaker picks up an unusual-looking vegetable —round, thick-skinned, and bright yellow. "What is this? A pepper!" he guesses. More laughter. "That's not a pepper. It's a tomato," says the grower. "Taste it!" The willing guinea pig takes a bite and pronounces it sweet. After gulping down the rest, he announces: "I love vegetables. I eat vegetables all the time. I eat lots of 'em."

"That's why you're so handsome," a bystander ribs back.

asparagus mixture. Return puree and reserved cooking liquid to pot. Add reserved asparagus tips, remaining green onions, the fresh dill, the white pepper and salt to taste. Simmer 3-4 minutes, until tips are just tender. Stir in cream, if desired. Taste soup, and adjust seasonings.
4. To serve, ladle into bowls and garnish with Parmesan and additional chopped fresh dill.

Sassy Mushrooms
3-4 servings

Cultivated white mushrooms are sold at groceries throughout all the seasons, but I buy them most often in the spring, when they're one of the relatively few vegetables that are available at the early farmers' markets. Inspired by a recipe from "The Vegetarian Epicure," Sassy Mushrooms simmer in a sauce of red wine and mustard that reduces to a succulent glaze. The results make a saucy side dish any time of the year.

1 pound fresh cultivated (white) mushrooms, whole
2 tablespoons butter
½ cup finely chopped onions or ¼ cup minced shallots
2 tablespoons Dijon-style mustard
2 tablespoons Worcestershire sauce
2 tablespoons maple syrup
⅔ cup dry red wine
¼ teaspoon salt
Freshly ground black pepper

1. Melt butter in large skillet. Add onions (or shallots). Cook gently, stirring occasionally, until translucent.
2. Meanwhile, combine mustard, Worcestershire sauce, maple syrup and red wine in a bowl. Stir in salt and a few grindings of pepper.
3. Gently rinse and drain mushrooms. Add mushrooms to cooked onions and cook over medium-high heat 3 minutes. Pour in wine mixture and simmer hard, stirring frequently, about 20 minutes, or until sauce is thickened and mushrooms are glistening. Season to taste with additional salt and pepper. Serve hot.

Celebration Salad with Morels, Radishes, and Spring Greens
6 servings

You could do this salad without the morels, but then it wouldn't be as much of a celebration, would it?

1 large head butterhead-type lettuce (Bibb or Buttercrunch)
1 bunch watercress
1 bunch radishes
½ pound morel mushrooms
½ pound cultivated (white) mushrooms
5 tablespoons olive oil, divided
2 teaspoons minced garlic
Juice of 1 lemon
Freshly ground black pepper

1. Tear lettuce and watercress apart into bite-size pieces. Rinse in cold water and dry thoroughly in a salad spinner or cotton towel. Clean radishes; cut into quarters. Combine greens and radishes in a large bowl and refrigerate until ready to use.
2. Clean morels by halving each one lengthwise and soaking them briefly in cold water. Rinse thoroughly and pat dry. Rinse the white mushrooms and halve or quarter them.
3. Warm 3 tablespoons olive oil and the garlic in a large skillet over low heat for 1 minute. Raise the heat to medium-high, add all the mushrooms, and sauté until barely tender, stirring often. Stir in lemon juice and remaining olive oil. Season with lots of freshly ground black pepper. (Can be held at this point, with the heat off, until ready to serve.)
4. To serve: warm the mushrooms briefly just before tossing with the greens. Portion onto salad plates and pass the pepper mill.

MORELS AND SHIITAKES

You've seen them at the farmers' market, those oddball mushrooms that remind you of small sponges or whimsical forest creatures. Morels have dark honeycombed caps atop thick white stems and are gathered wild from the woods, from spots kept carefully secret. They're around for a just few weeks in May, when weather conditions are right for their ripening. If spring comes on too dry or too warm, the crop will be minimal, but even in years when the crop is plentiful, morels fetch up to $25 a pound at farmers' markets. No wonder the gathering places are kept a mystery.

Shiitakes look less imposing, more elegant—a smooth, brown, somewhat flattish head on an elongated stem. Some say they have a garlic-pine aroma that signals their freshness. Shiitake spores are planted inside oak logs, watered regularly to maintain proper moisture levels, and harvested about every six months. More affordable than morels, shiitakes are finding their way into many farmers' markets.

Morels and shiitakes are enjoying great popularity as the foodie boom continues in the United States. Their earthy flavor and meaty texture are as special and satisfying as fresh seafood. The simplest preparations involve quick sautéing and modest additions like garlic and fresh herbs. Inspired cooks, however, combine them with cream or wine, simmer them in stews and soups, and use them to accent other special products like salmon and fresh asparagus.

Italian Marinated Mushrooms
4 servings

Think of this one when you first bring out the grill in late spring, for Italian Marinated Mushrooms are good to nibble on while you're waiting for the chops or chicken. They're also great mixed with chopped fresh basil or oregano. Try them on an antipasto platter or in a tossed salad.

This recipe came from the Time-Life cookbook series, "Foods of the World." I couldn't find a way to improve the flavor, but I did cut down on the oil and I took out the salt. I often use Italian Marinated Mushrooms as an ingredient in other dishes, such as the Bistro Leek Salad on page 57.

1 pound fresh cultivated (white) mushrooms
4 tablespoons olive oil
Juice of two lemons
2 bay leaves
2 large garlic cloves, smashed
6 whole black peppercorns

1. Gently rinse the mushrooms and let drain. Halve or leave whole.
2. In a large stainless steel frying pan, combine all the ingredients (except the mushrooms) with ½ cup water. Bring to a boil. Reduce to a simmer, cover pan and cook 10 minutes.
3. Add mushrooms and simmer uncovered 5 minutes, stirring often. Remove from heat and allow mushrooms to cool in the liquid. Continue to marinate one or more hours at room temperature, or up to two days in the refrigerator, tossing occasionally. Serve at room temperature after draining off the marinade.

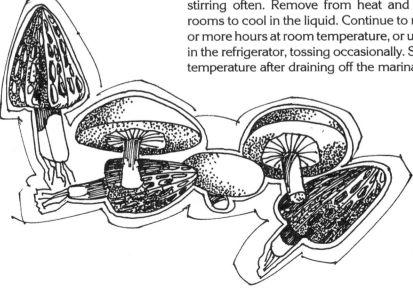

Grilled Steak-Wrapped Scallion Appetizers
Makes 32-36 bite-size appetizers

Very easy and very good. You'll need large, thin slices of top-quality round steak for this recipe: have the butcher do it on a meat slicer.

1 **pound top round steak, sliced horizontally about ¼-inch thick (4-5 slices total)**
1 **bunch thick green onions, root ends and about one half of the green tops trimmed off**
⅓ **cup soy sauce**
¼ **cup bottled salsa**
2 **teaspoons minced garlic, mashed to a paste**

1. Tightly roll meat slices around the green onions. Secure each with a toothpick and place in a flat, shallow dish just large enough to hold the rolls.
2. Mix soy sauce, salsa and garlic paste and pour over the steak; let marinate at room temperature one hour (or in refrigerator 2-3 hours), turning often.
3. Meanwhile, prepare coals on an outdoor grill. Grill steak rolls 3-4 minutes per side. Remove toothpicks and cut rolls into ½-inch rounds—an electric knife does this neatly and quickly. Serve hot or at room temperature.

"The value of local food is that it contributes to a sense of place. Part of this is intangible: a kind of sentimental value simply in knowing that one's meals come from nearby. But what is more important to perceptive diners is that foods from different places taste different. And diversity in taste is probably the most interesting part of eating."

Edward Behr,
"The Artful Eater,"
1992

THE SEASONS THEY GO 'ROUND AND 'ROUND
The Dane County Farmers' Market in Madison

There's not a market in the Midwest that can outshine the Wisconsin state capital's for food quality, product diversity, crowd size and plain old, people-watching good fun. Every Saturday morning from the end of April to early November, up to twenty thousand bag-and basket-toting market lovers throng the sidewalks that ring the stately domed capitol in downtown Madison.

Madison's may be the most entertaining of all Wisconsin markets. It's an eye-opening, mouth-watering, neck-craning adventure of sound, scent, color, taste and motion. However, just who's being entertained and who's doing the entertaining is not always clear: everyone plays a role. It's a weekly circle game, an ever-changing crazy quilt of buyers and sellers together in an oddly synchronized slow-dance, the vendors forming a benevolent corral around a counter-clockwise parade of strolling shoppers.

The Madison market hums and buzzes with deals made, greetings shouted, questions asked, gossip traded. Sometimes music is playing: soft guitar strums or maybe the blast of a circus organ. Inviting smells hover at nose-level, changing as you pass each stand—a faint trace of apple, a sharp hit of basil, next a wave of chocolate, and—oh, someone must be frying sweet peppers in butter. Breakfast is served, sample by sample: cubes of cheese, chunks of melon, sips of cider. You can fill up without spending a penny.

Colors tell the season. In spring, the greens reign: asparagus, lettuce, bedding plants, watercress, fiddlehead ferns, all under a giant green canopy of over two dozen tree varieties. In summer, it's a riot of brightness and intensity: purple peppers, blood red tomatoes, snow white cauliflower, a rainbow of gladiolas. Autumn comes in gold glory with pumpkins and apples and onions and potatoes. When bad weather brings out colorful, bobbing umbrellas, even the rain has a hard time dampening the richness of this market.

The astounding scope and success of the Dane County Farmers' Market is a tribute to the cooperative efforts made by those who started it in 1972, and to those who carefully tend it today.

Ron Jensen, a Farm Management agent with the Dane County Extension back in the early '70s, knew what a weekly market could mean to area farmers and Madison consumers. He worked with Jonathan Barry (then a farmer, eventually the County Executive) to find a location for the market.

Turned down by area shopping malls, they got a better reaction from the Central Madison Committee, which was connected to the Chamber of Commerce. Both the Chamber and the Mayor's office saw the farmers' market as a means to revitalize Madison's downtown, still suffering from the Vietnam War protest years. Both groups were eager to lend a hand in making the market happen.

Madison has a reputation for being slow-as-snails when it comes to city development projects, but this wasn't the case with the farmers' market. Permits and insurance were quickly

secured and the market was on.

An unqualified hit, the Madison market began to grow immediately. By 1975, a second market, open on Wednesdays, was flourishing just off the Capitol Square. In 1976, a non-profit, grower-based corporation was organized to manage the markets. Through the years, many annual special events have become tied to Dane County's market: June's Cows on the Concourse; a Fall Harvest Tasting; various sports competitions; indoor holiday markets at the Civic Center; and more.

Today, the Dane County Farmers' Market remains an organization whose services are strictly defined and highly regulated. Products must be Wisconsin-produced; crafts and any goods not grown or produced by the seller are not allowed. An eight-page brochure outlining market policies and approved sale items accompany stall applications. If you don't comply, you're out.

With all the regulations, one might think this market could get boring, stilted. But of course, just the opposite is true (see "A Taste of Madison," page 151). Dane County's is the ultimate in farmers' markets; and once you've been there, you'll be 'round and 'round again.

Fresh Market
W·I·S·C·O·N·S·I·N

SUMMER VEGETABLES

Bacon-Fried Green Beans
4-6 servings

I met Gene Garbowski at a Wisconsin Fresh Market Vegetable Growers' Association conference. Like many growers, he was lightly amused by my request for written-down recipes. "It's all in my head," he said. Gene did recite his method for Bacon-Fried Green Beans—sans measurements, of course. I hope he doesn't mind that I slipped in a few cups and tablespoons for the less experienced.

Note: One-half cup chopped bell (sweet) peppers may be substituted for the banana peppers, which are on the spicy side.

4 slices bacon
1 pound green beans, ends trimmed off, blanched (see page 21)
1 banana pepper, chopped
1 tablespoon flour
Salt and freshly ground black pepper

Chop bacon into 1-inch pieces and fry in a pan until crispy. Add beans and peppers; cook over medium heat about 3 minutes, stirring often. Sprinkle in flour, then stir in several tablespoons water to make a gravy (add water until desired consistency is reached). Season to taste with salt and pepper.

Gene Garbowski
Brussels, Wisconsin

Crock Dill Pickles
Yields about 1 gallon

"Every grandmother in the neighborhood used this recipe when I was a kid," comments Carol Schlei of Mahn's Farm Market in Oak Creek. Once you've made them, you'll know why: no home-canning hassles and plenty of spunky flavor. I made these crunchy, low calorie, low cost and no cholesterol treats for an annual family reunion one summer, and the entire gallon was gone within 24 hours. (Now I know better than to bring the whole gallon along.)

MEASURELESSLY GOOD

By trade, most farmers are casual cooks—there's just not enough hours in the day to fuss with elaborate dishes, strict measurements and extra pots and pans. Or recipes themselves, for that matter. When asked to send in original recipes for this cookbook, lots of folks chuckled at the thought of writing down what mostly comes automatically to them.

Once, a tanned, grinning gentleman selling sweet peppers at a market revealed his stir-fry recipe: "Step 1, walk out into the garden and see what's ready. Step 2, pick it. Step 3, fry it up."

He did go on to brag that he was the "Stir-fry Master," so you'd think there had to be a bit more to it. Sure enough, when pressed, he started talking about fresh ginger root, garlic and "maybe just a splash of something potent." But write it down? No way. He's probably never done it the same way twice.

IN A PICKLE

Making pickles? For best results, use pickling cucumbers; they are grown specifically for pickling, having a smaller size and retaining crispness better than "slicing" cucumbers. Add a bit of alum to the pickling solution. It's used to keep pickles firm and is available at well-stocked groceries or drugstores. (Better yet, pinch some from your neighbor rather than buying a whole jar.)

Crock Dill Pickles are at their healthiest and tastiest when they are about three to four days old, before the salty brine has completely infused the cucumbers. But if you like your pickles strong, go ahead and let them soak longer. Either way, once they've reached the just-right stage, refrigerate them to slow down the souring process.

This recipe can be easily doubled.

½ **gallon soft water**
¼ **cup pickling salt**
¾ **cup mild vinegar (5% acidity) or cider vinegar**
4 pounds (about 50-60) small pickling cucumbers
Two large budding dill plant heads OR 1 bunch fresh dill sprigs
A 1-gallon glass wide-mouth jar or crockery bowl, cleaned thoroughly
½ **teaspoon powdered alum**
2 large cloves fresh garlic, thinly sliced

1. Combine water, pickling salt and vinegar in a pot; boil briefly. Keep warm.
2. Meanwhile, scrub cucumbers well and pack into jar or bowl, with dill at the bottom and top. Sprinkle in alum and distribute garlic slices throughout.
3. Pour warm brine over cucumbers. Place a plate over cucumbers and weight with a clean rock or other heavy item to hold the pickles in the brine. Store in a cool place for 2-4 days until pickles reach desired degree of doneness. Keep refrigerated after this point to prolong the flavor.
4. Note: If pickles are left in the crock too long or are not kept cool enough, they may develop a scum on the top and get soft. If you notice this beginning to happen, repack pickles into sealable containers along with the brine and dill, and refrigerate.

Carol Schlei
Mahn's Farm Market
Oak Creek, Wisconsin

Linguine with Cauliflower, Garlic and Hot Red Pepper
4 servings

Don't you love the display of snowy white cauliflower at the farmers' market? Giant flower heads collared in queenly green—they really beckon the shopper. Here's a superb way to treat fresh cauliflower. It's a make-over of a recipe from an Italian restaurant called Pasta Nostra in Connecticut. It works as a side dish but is easily good enough for the main event. If you're watching your cholesterol, substitute margarine or additional olive oil for the butter.

1 large cauliflower (about 1 ½ pounds)
3 tablespoons olive oil, divided
2 tablespoons butter
1 ½ cups thinly sliced onions
2 teaspoons minced garlic
3 plum tomatoes, chopped
¼ cup chopped fresh parsley
¼ cup chopped fresh oregano OR 2 teaspoons dried oregano
½ teaspoon red pepper flakes (or more to taste)
Salt and freshly ground black pepper
6 ounces dried linguine
¼ cup freshly grated Parmesan or Romano cheese

1. Cut cauliflower into small flowerets. Heat 2 tablespoons olive oil and the butter in a very large skillet. Add cauliflower; sauté over medium-high heat, stirring often, until lightly browned, about 10 minutes. Transfer cauliflower to a large bowl.
2. Melt remaining olive oil in the pan; add onions and garlic. Cover and cook over medium heat until soft, stirring often.
3. Add tomatoes, parsley and oregano to pan. Stir in reserved cauliflower and pepper flakes. Season with salt and pepper to taste. Cook 10-15 minutes longer, until cauliflower is tender. (Can be held at this time and reheated later, but take care not to overcook the cauliflower.)
4. To serve: Cook linguine until just tender in lots of boiling, salted water. Warm a large bowl in oven or near the stove. Drain pasta, reserving a little of the liquid. Toss pasta with cauliflower and grated cheese in the warm bowl. (If it is too dry, toss in some of the reserved pasta water.) Season with more black pepper to taste.

"Cauliflower is nothing but cabbage with a college education."

Mark Twain

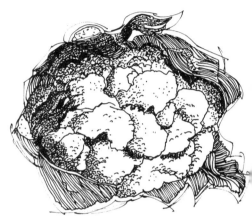

Sweet and Hot Pepper Frittata
2-3 servings

Baby vegetables never reached the fad stage here in Wisconsin, but one grower found a unique way to market them. Linda Fuentes, whose main business is full-sized organic produce, has an eager young son named Adrian who's been known to set up his own small stand beside hers. His specialties include pint-sized cabbages, tiny tomatoes and green peppers the size of golf balls, with tiny prices to match. Adrian hawks his wares with a sweet voice and a knowing eye: "Wouldn't you like some of my baby vegetables? Best in the market!" Who can resist?

Here's his mom's recipe for Sweet and Hot Pepper Frittata, an open-face, vegetable-stuffed omelette—just right for using some of Adrian's best babies.

1 tablespoon olive oil
¾ cup thinly sliced bell peppers, any color or any combination of colors
1 small jalapeño pepper, seeded and chopped
¼ cup diced onion
1 clove garlic, halved
1 small tomato, seeded and chopped
4 eggs
¼ teaspoon paprika
⅛ teaspoon salt
2 tablespoons freshly grated Parmesan cheese

1. Heat oil in a 9- or 10-inch skillet, nonstick if possible. Add sweet and hot peppers, onion and garlic. Sauté 3 minutes over medium heat, then remove garlic.
2. Add tomatoes to skillet. Cook 3 more minutes, stirring occasionally. Do not allow vegetables to brown.
3. Beat eggs with 2 tablespoons water, paprika and salt. Pour into pan, cover, and cook over medium-low heat until set, 5-8 minutes. If the top is too wet, slide the frittata onto a large plate, place the hot pan over the top and turn frittata back into the pan. It will only take another moment to finish the cooking. To serve, slide frittata back onto the plate, sprinkle with Parmesan and serve hot or at room temperature, cut into wedges.

Linda Fuentes
Harmony Valley Farm
Viroqua, Wisconsin

Middle Eastern Stuffed Tomatoes
4 servings

Mideast meets Midwest when you stuff local vine-ripened tomatoes with couscous and the sunny flavors of garlic, mint, lemon juice and imported olives. Couscous is a Middle Eastern staple—tiny grains of semolina pasta that cook up quickly and easily. Although rice could be substituted, couscous is usually available in larger grocery stores and cooperatives. It's worth looking for.

1½ cups chicken stock or water
4 teaspoons olive oil, divided
1 cup couscous
6 medium tomatoes
3 tablespoons pitted, chopped imported black olives (Greek or kalamatas work well)
Juice of ½ lemon
1 teaspoon minced garlic mashed to a paste with ¼ teaspoon salt
2 tablespoons chopped fresh parsley
2 tablespoons chopped fresh mint OR 1 tablespoon dried mint
Freshly ground black pepper

1. Prepare couscous by bringing 1½ cups chicken stock or water to boil. Stir in 1 teaspoon olive oil and the couscous. Turn off heat. Cover pan and let stand 5 minutes. Remove cover, fluff couscous with fork, and cool to room temperature.
2. To prepare tomatoes: slice off the top of four of them; remove and discard seeds. Scoop out most of the pulp; chop pulp coarsely. Drain the tomato shells upside down for a few minutes. Halve and seed the remaining two tomatoes; chop coarsely.
3. Combine all the chopped tomatoes with the cooled couscous, olives, lemon juice, remaining 3 teaspoons olive oil, garlic/salt paste, parsley, mint and pepper to taste. If desired, let the ingredients marinate an hour or two to develop flavor. Spoon into tomatoes just before serving.

BASICS IN BRIEF: KITCHEN AIDS

● To pit olives: Place on cutting board. Lay the flat part of a wide-bladed knife over each olive and smack it with the base of your hand. They will split open for easy pitting.

● For juicier lemons: Roll and press lemons against work surface before juicing them.

● To peel garlic cloves: Follow directions given above for pitting olives.

● To make garlic paste: Chop cloves coarsely, sprinkle on a little salt or pepper, then press and mash with a fork or the flat of a knife.

SELLING POINTS

"I thought at first that I would last only a week, but there is a mesmerism in the selling, in the coins and the bills, the all-day touching of hands. I am often in charge of the peppers, and, like everyone else behind the tables by our truck, I can look at a plastic sack of them now and tell its weight."

"A coin will sink faster through bell peppers than it will through water. When people lose their money they go after it like splashing bears. Peppers everywhere. Peppers two deep over the apples, three deep over the plums. Peppers all over the ground."

"There is a rhythm in the movement of the crowd, in the stopping, the selecting, the moving on— the time unconsciously budgeted to assess one farm against another, to convict a tomato, to choose a peach. The seller comes to feel the rate of flow, and—for all the small remarks, the meeting of eyes—to feel as well the seclusion of anonymity that come with the money aprons and the hanging scales."

From
"Giving Good Weight,"
by John McPhee, 1979

Fresh Freezer Salsa
Makes 8-10 cups

A batch of homemade salsa captures all the best the farmers' market can offer: fresh, seasonal flavors; colorful, healthy eating; economy; and ease of preparation. This recipe is from Sharon Cybart and Lyman Fuson of Fertile Ground Farm in Brooklyn, Wisconsin. Says Sharon: "The only problem we have with it is that we eat it so fast when it's fresh that we're never able to put enough in the freezer to last all winter!"

10-15 medium tomatoes
1 large onion
2 medium bell peppers (any color)
3-6 fresh hot peppers to taste (jalapeños or serranos are best)
½ cup cider vinegar
¼ cup minced cilantro (fresh coriander)
¾ teaspoon salt

Finely chop tomatoes and set in colander to drain. Finely dice onion and bell peppers. Mince the hot peppers (it's a good idea to do this with plastic gloves on). Combine all ingredients and let stand 1 hour to allow flavors to develop. Add more minced hot pepper if it's not spicy enough. Eat salsa fresh or freeze it. (It will be juicier, but just as tasty after it is thawed.)

Sharon Cybart and Lyman Fuson
Fertile Ground Farm
Brooklyn, Wisconsin

Spicy Corn Kernel Cake
4 servings

"Cake" in this recipe refers to the shape, and not the texture of the dish. Fresh corn kernels, bits of green onion and minced hot peppers are pressed into a sizzling hot skillet. Baked until a crunchy crust forms to hold the shape, the cake is then cut into wedges and served with salsa. The idea for this easy and clever way to serve fresh corn came from James McNair's "Corn Cookbook." You can skip the hot stuff, and/or add bits of ham or sweet red peppers to the mixture.

Note: Don't make this without a heavy (preferably cast iron), ovenproof skillet; lighter-gauge pans will make the cake scorch.

2 tablespoons vegetable oil
2 heaping cups fresh corn kernels (cut from about 6 ears)
2 tablespoons minced fresh basil, cilantro (fresh coriander) or parsley
2 tablespoons minced green onion
1-2 tablespoons minced hot pepper (try jalapeño or serrano)
3 tablespoons cornmeal
3 tablespoons flour
Salt and freshly ground black pepper to taste
Fresh basil, cilantro or parsley leaves, for garnish
Freshly made or bottled salsa

1. Preheat oven to 400 degrees. Measure oil into a medium skillet and heat in oven 25-30 minutes.
2. Combine remaining ingredients except the last two in a bowl, then press evenly into the hot pan. Bake 25-30 minutes, until edges are brown and crispy.
3. Run a spatula around the outer rim of, and underneath, the corn cake to loosen it from the pan. Wearing hot pads, place a heat-proof serving plate face down over the pan and invert the pan so the cake falls onto the plate. Garnish with fresh herbs and serve with salsa.

BASICS IN BRIEF: PEELING, SEEDING AND FREEZING TOMATOES

It seems unfair that during a few short weeks of the summer we are inundated with our favorite garden vegetable, while during the long months of winter we're faced with the mealy texture and flat taste of shipped and store-bought tomatoes. So enjoy garden-fresh tomatoes as long as you can and in as many different ways as you can. And carry a little of that red-ripe flavor into the colder months by freezing your surplus.

It's easy to peel and seed tomatoes for freezing or for recipes that require genuine—not canned—tomato flavor. First, cut out the cores and make a small "X" with a sharp or serrated knife in the bottom of each tomato. Dip in boiling water for 10-30 seconds (the riper the tomato, the shorter the time). Cool under gently running water. The skins will now slip off easily. To seed, cut the tomatoes in half horizontally; squeeze out the seeds, or scoop them out with your finger. The tomatoes can now be chopped or pureed, then frozen or used as required.

Tomato Corn Casserole
4-6 servings

The world's a happy place when tomatoes and corn are in season.

2 tablespoons butter or olive oil
½ cup minced onion
1 cup wheat germ or dried breadcrumbs
2 cups fresh corn kernels
Salt and freshly ground black pepper
3 tomatoes, sliced
3 tablespoons light or heavy cream
Bacon bits (optional, but if you use them use real ones only, please)

1. Melt butter or heat oil in medium skillet; add onion and cook slowly until translucent.
2. Stir in wheat germ or breadcrumbs. Cook over medium heat, stirring often, until mixture looks and smells toasted.
3. Spread half the corn in a medium baking dish and sprinkle with salt and pepper. Cover with half the tomato slices, then spread half the onion/wheat germ mixture evenly over tomatoes. Add the remaining corn, then season with more salt and pepper. Drizzle cream evenly over this, then top with remaining tomatoes and onion/wheat germ mixture. Can be held at this point until ready to bake.
4. To bake: Preheat oven to 350 degrees. Bake casserole 30 minutes. If desired, sprinkle with bacon bits and bake 5 minutes longer. Serve hot.

Hushpuppy Eggplant
6 servings, and also yields 8-10 corn muffins

Pat Matthews of the Eau Claire Farmers' Market borrowed this down-home recipe from "Grandma's Cookbook." Sliced eggplant is dipped in a cornmeal batter, pan-fried, sprinkled with shredded Cheddar and served hot. "This is so sweet and crunchy," says Pat, "Plus there are the muffins as a bonus." The leftover batter is baked into muffins that make your next morning's breakfast a snap— if they last that long!

2 cups cornmeal
1 cup flour
½ cup sugar
1 teaspoon baking powder
1 teaspoon salt
2 tablespoons melted butter
1½ cups milk, plus additional milk to thin batter
3 tablespoons vegetable oil, plus additional oil to sauté eggplant
1 egg
1½ pounds eggplant
½ cup grated Cheddar cheese

1. Prepare batter by mixing the first five ingredients in a large bowl. In a separate bowl, mix melted butter, 1½ cups milk, 3 tablespoons oil, and the egg. Add the wet mixture to the dry and stir until well combined.
2. Peel and slice eggplant ¼ inch thick.
3. Heat 1½ tablespoons oil in a non-stick skillet. Dip eggplant slices in batter and arrange in pan without overcrowding it. Cook over medium heat until egg-plant is tender and golden brown on both sides. Sprinkle cooked eggplant with grated Cheddar and remove to a warm place. Repeat this process until all the eggplant slices are cooked. (If batter gets too thick, stir in additional milk.) Serve warm.
4. To bake muffins: Preheat oven to 375 degrees. Divide remaining cornbread batter into a greased or paper-lined muffin tin. Bake 20-25 minutes, until toothpick inserted in center of muffins comes out clean.

Pat Matthews
Eau Claire Farmers' Market

WHEN TOO MUCH OF GOOD THING IS GREAT

Ever wonder about the mounds of fresh produce still left at the end of a busy market day? No matter what the season, there's usually some unsold food getting packed back into the trucks and vans, bound for another market or, just as often, the compost heap.

Some farmers, however, have found a way to let the produce that would otherwise go to waste be put to a very good use. They donate their still-fresh leftovers to places which in turn pass the food on to those in need.

It's a very simple idea, sensible and generous, too. Sometimes the farmers themselves drop off the food at area churches or shelter homes. In some Wisconsin towns, more systematic programs are in place.

At the Wednesday farmers' market in Madison, volunteers from the Atwood Community Center pass out empty boxes to vendors at the end of the day. They fill a truck with free produce that is then distributed at the center's weekly food pantry. Beloit's Harbor for the Homeless, a shelter program, uses the donated produce to feed its

participants. In West Allis, members of Christian Garden Harvest go from stall to stall to pick up whatever farmers will contribute.

What about you? Do you notice "too much of a good thing" at your market? Contact a local social service organization or your market manager to see what can be done.

HOW TO COOK BULGUR

Bulgur is easy to prepare: pour boiling water (1½ parts water to 1 part bulgur) over it, stir, cover and let soak 15-20 minutes. Fluff with a fork when all the water is absorbed.

Bulgur Caponatina
Makes 6 cups

Here's a rendition of caponata, a versatile Italian eggplant dish that's served as a relish, salad, side dish or stuffing. This version adds nutritious bulgur, a processed wheat best known as the main ingredient in tabbuli. Loaded with eggplant and other fresh market produce, Bulgur Caponatina has rich flavor and no cholesterol.

The recipe comes from a cookbook called "Grains," put out by Bright Eye Farm in Door County. Author Toni Christenson, who operates a farm market in Jacksonport, suggests these uses: "Hot over garlic bread or cold as a sandwich layer. It can also be antipasto or mixed with shredded lettuce for a salad, or plain as a complement to fish, fowl or meat." It's also great as part of a cheese melt, in an omelette, or on crackers with lemon juice.

2 tablespoons olive oil
½ cup finely chopped onion
½ cup finely chopped celery
1 or 2 eggplants (1½ pounds total), peeled and cubed
1 medium bell pepper (red or green), thinly sliced
2 teaspoons minced garlic
⅓ cup pine nuts, lightly toasted
½ cup stuffed green olives, chopped
2 medium tomatoes, seeded and chopped
1 cup cooked bulgur (½ cup raw soaked with ¾ cup water—see side bar)
¼ cup cider vinegar or red wine vinegar
2-3 tablespoons chopped fresh basil
2 tablespoons honey
Salt and freshly ground black pepper to taste

1. Heat oil in wok or large skillet. Add onion, celery, eggplant, bell peppers and garlic; cook over medium-high heat, stirring and tossing, until vegetables are limp, about 10 minutes.
2. Add remaining ingredients and continue to cook 4-5 minutes longer. Taste and adjust seasonings. Serve hot or at room temperature. It will keep in the refrigerator in glass jars for two weeks.

Toni Christenson
Bright Eye Farm Market
Jacksonport, Wisconsin

Grilled Eggplant, Cherry Tomato and Romaine Toss
4 main-course servings, 6-8 as dinner salad

Just as it soaks up oil in a pan, the sponge-like nature of eggplant soaks up the smoky flavor of the grill. This salad combines strips of barbecued eggplant with cherry tomatoes, Parmesan cheese, crisp romaine lettuce and a garlicky herb dressing.

Dressing:

1 teaspoon minced garlic, mashed to paste with ¼ teaspoon salt
2 tablespoons chopped fresh lemon thyme (or substitute other fresh herb)
2 tablespoons red wine vinegar
1 egg white
4 tablespoons olive oil
Freshly ground black pepper

Salad:

1 whole eggplant (about 1 pound)
Olive oil to brush on eggplant
Salt and freshly ground black pepper
1 large head romaine lettuce
12-15 cherry tomatoes, halved
¼-½ cup freshly grated Parmesan cheese

1. To make dressing: Combine first four dressing ingredients, then whisk in olive oil in a thin stream. Season with pepper to taste. Set aside until ready to use.
2. Heat coals on a small, kettle-type grill. Slice off a 3-inch piece of eggplant skin from two opposite sides of its rounded middle. (This will create a flat edge for grilling.) Now cut eggplant lengthwise into four thick wedges. Brush each with olive oil and grill (covered) 3-4 minutes per side, or until very tender. Cool to room temperature and slice eggplant into 3-inch strips. Season to taste with salt and pepper.
3. Chop and clean lettuce. Dry in salad spinner or towels.
4. To serve, toss lettuce, eggplant, tomatoes, Parmesan and dressing in a large bowl. Season with additional pepper.

EASY-COME, EASY-GO WAYS WITH VEGETABLES

Here's some ideas that will come easy for you, and will make your vegetables go fast.

• Parboil **leeks** until barely tender; drain and pat dry. Slice into rounds and toss with homemade or bottled Italian dressing.

• Add a garlic clove, some lemon juice and a little olive oil to water in a pot, then steam **broccoli** over it.

• Sprinkle freshly cooked **asparagus** spears with lemon juice and dill, or lime juice and chopped cilantro (fresh coriander).

• Mix a little horseradish with yogurt or sour cream; dollop on sautéed **zucchini** rounds.

• Peel and thickly slice large white **onions**; brush with a vinegar/oil/herb marinade and grill on both sides until charred and tender.

• Sprinkle chopped hard-cooked egg or toasted breadcrumbs over steamed **cauliflower**.

• Toast sesame seeds or whole cumin seeds in a cast iron pan and add to salads, cole slaws or cooked vegetables.

• Spike a stir-fried vegetable (sliced bell peppers, zucchini sticks, green beans, eggplant cubes, etc.) with red pepper flakes and grated ginger root.

FROM THE CABBAGE PATCH

Cabbage is a big-hearted vegetable, each head generous in nutrition and value. And there's a lot of it around at market time. Wisconsin is a major cabbage state, growing some 5000 acres a year. What is there to do with all that cabbage? In soups or salads, as cole slaw or sauerkraut, for stuffing and in just about everything but dessert, cabbage is one the most versatile vegetables around.

Common roundhead green cabbage loves the cool Wisconsin weather. Early, midseason and fall varieties are found at markets throughout the state. Other tasty members of the cabbage family include: red cabbage, with a bright color and crisp texture; curly-leaved Savoys, a decorative alternative to common cabbage, great for stuffing purposes; pak-choi (or bok choy); and Chinese cabbage. The last two are used extensively in oriental cooking.

All raw cabbages take well to stir-frying. Place a wok or heavy pan over high heat for a few minutes, add a small amount of oil, then toss and cook shredded or chopped cabbage briefly, until it begins to wilt just a bit. Add soy sauce, minced garlic, grated fresh ginger, green onions and bits of ham, or any additions that please you.

Sesame Slaw
8 servings

This cole slaw has an oriental bend, with red pepper, green onions and the exotic flavor of dark sesame oil.

1 small head (1-1½ pounds) green or red cabbage
½ cup red bell pepper slivers or shredded carrots
½ cup finely minced green onions
3 tablespoons red wine vinegar
2 teaspoons olive oil
1 teaspoon dark sesame oil
2 teaspoons sugar
½ teaspoon salt
¼ teaspoon crushed red pepper flakes (optional)
½ cup toasted walnuts, coarsely chopped

Core and quarter cabbage. Shred or slice it thinly. Combine with remaining ingredients (except nuts); marinate in the refrigerator for at least one hour, tossing occasionally. Top with toasted walnuts just before serving.

Cheesy Zucchini
3-4 servings

This is a really simple side dish. Add a few shrimp with the zucchini and you've got a great main course. If you'd rather use fresh herbs in this recipe, double the amounts given for dried. Try different types of cheese, too.

1 tablespoon butter or margarine
3-4 small zucchini (about 1 pound total)
1 teaspoon dried basil
1 teaspoon dried oregano
2 tomatoes, sliced
½ cup shredded Mozzarella cheese

1. Heat butter or margarine in medium skillet. Slice zucchini into rounds and add to butter. Toss 3 minutes over medium-high heat.
2. Add basil and oregano, and continue to toss and cook another few minutes until just tender.
3. Place sliced tomatoes over zucchini, sprinkle on the cheese, cover and heat until cheese is melted.

Mary O'Grady
Sun Prairie Farmers' Market

Patty Pan in a Pan
4 servings

Here's another summer squash recipe from Mary O'Grady of Sun Prairie. She says: "I like using my cast iron skillet when I make this; it gives the dish a special flavor and keeps the squash nice and warm."

2 tablespoons olive oil
1-2 teaspoons minced garlic
2 large or 6 small patty pan squash (about 1 pound), sliced
4 large leaves fresh basil, chopped (or use any fresh herb)
6 cherry tomatoes, halved
Salt and freshly ground black pepper

1. Heat oil in cast iron skillet. Add garlic and sliced patty pan.
2. Toss and cook over medium high heat several minutes, until just tender.
3. Stir in chopped basil and cherry tomatoes; heat through. Season to taste with salt and pepper; serve hot directly from the pan.

Mary O'Grady
Sun Prairie Farmers' Market

A FARM MARKET WITH ALL THE TRIMMINGS
The Elegant Farmer, Mukwonago

Roadside stands can be as unpretentious as a picnic table temporarily covered with tomatoes, set on a front lawn with a bucket nearby to collect coins. The barking of the family dog is the farmer's signal that a customer has arrived. At the other end of the farm market spectrum lie the big operations that are open most of the year and lure buyers with much more than ripe tomatoes. One of the grandest of these Wisconsin farm markets is The Elegant Farmer in Mukwonago, west of Milwaukee.

Nearly every type of food grown or produced in Wisconsin is available at The Elegant Farmer. No barking dogs needed here—it is as much tourist attraction as food source, with highway billboards heralding the plenty from miles away. In spring, bedding plants by the thousands line the parking lots to beckon motorists. You can imagine what it looks like during summer and fall harvest times.

Inside is a complete food shopping mall: aisles of local and shipped-in produce, fresh or frozen; a not-to-be-missed candy store; a gift-and-book shop; dried herbs and spice bins; a bakery famous for giant fruit muffins, Schaum tortes, and fresh apple pies baked in brown bags; a turkey/butcher shop ("Your Complete Turkey Store"); packaged goods from mustards to maple syrup; and a full-scale delicatessen.

"In the summer, you can't get through the aisles around here," says Dolores Sikora, chef and manager of the deli. Crowd-haters, however, can take advantage of the pick-your-own operations offered in nearby fields. At The Elegant Farmer, there really is something for everyone.

Salad-In-A-Sandwich
3-4 lunch-size servings, twice that as side dish

A loaf of crusty French bread soaks up all the fresh and exciting flavors in this salad-in-a-sandwich. It's loaded with good things like sweet peppers, tomatoes, olives, red onions, garlic and basil, but you'll probably think of other additions you can't skip as you cruise the market stands. Serve it with lasagne or Italian spaghetti, as picnic fare, or for a summer lunch.

2 teaspoons minced garlic
½ teaspoon cracked black pepper
1 can (2 ounces) anchovy fillets, well drained
1 tablespoon balsamic or red wine vinegar
2 tablespoons olive oil
⅔ cup coarsely chopped stuffed green olives, Greek olives, or a combination
1 long loaf French bread
1 small red onion, thinly sliced
1 medium green bell pepper, thinly sliced
1 medium red bell pepper, thinly sliced
2 medium tomatoes, sliced
Additional vinegar, olive oil and cracked black pepper
2 tablespoons chopped fresh basil or pesto (optional)

1. In a medium bowl, mash garlic and ½ teaspoon cracked black pepper with a fork until a paste is formed. Coarsely chop anchovies and mash them into the garlic paste. Stir in vinegar, olive oil and chopped olives.
2. Slice bread loaf in half horizontally and pull out some of the inside bread from each half. (Bread scraps can be used to make croutons, dried for breadcrumbs or donated to the birds.) Place bottom half of loaf on a large sheet of aluminum foil and spread olive mixture evenly over bread surface. Layer onions, peppers and tomatoes over this.
3. Sprinkle additional vinegar, olive oil and black pepper on the cut surface of the top bread half. Sprinkle with chopped basil or spread with pesto, if available. Place it on the stacked sandwich; press down firmly.
4. Wrap the loaf securely in the aluminum foil and weight it with whatever heavy articles are available: books, cans, etc. Keep it weighted one hour or longer. Refrigeration isn't necessary unless it won't be served for several hours. To serve, remove foil, insert tooth-picks along the length of the loaf, and slice. The sandwich tastes best at room temperature.

Grill Salad
4 main course servings

This may be the quintessential summer salad. Choose your favorite bounty from the market, pair it with lean beef or chicken breasts, marinate the ingredients and grill over hot coals for smoky summer flavor. Grill Salad should be served slightly warm or at room temperature; just add crusty french bread, a glass of wine or iced tea and a cool evening breeze.

1 pound boneless top round sirloin (in one piece about 1½ inches thick) OR two 8-ounce boneless, skinless chicken breasts

6-8 cups assorted vegetables, cut into equal-size chunks for skewering, such as: zucchini, eggplant, bell peppers, onion, mushrooms, cherry tomatoes or parboiled potatoes

1 head romaine lettuce, cleaned, dried and torn into bite-size pieces

Freshly ground black pepper

Meat Marinade:

1 teaspoon minced garlic, mashed to a paste
½ cup soy sauce
2 tablespoons wine vinegar
2 tablespoons olive oil
¼ cup salsa (optional)

Vegetable Marinade:

¼ cup wine vinegar
2 teaspoons dried thyme or basil
1 tablespoon Dijon-style mustard
½ teaspoon salt
⅔ cup olive or salad oil

1. To marinate meat: Combine meat marinade ingredients in a glass dish just large enough to hold the meat. Place meat in marinade and turn several times to coat well. Cover and refrigerate 1-3 hours, turning occasionally.

2. To marinate vegetables: Combine vinegar, herb, mustard and salt in a large bowl. Slowly whisk in oil. Toss vegetable chunks in the marinade until lightly coated. Leave unrefrigerated, tossing occasionally, for as long as the meat marinates.

"I've heard home cooks speak with annoyance of recipes that 'don't work.' And I'm sure some don't. But modern cooks often misunderstand the nature of a recipe. They tend to mistake it for the dish itself, although a recipe is a notation, an outline, a fluid thing. The dish takes its definite form only from the ingredients at hand and from the adjustments made by the cook, according to his or her particular skill and understanding. Scarcely any recipe can or should yield a fixed result.

Edward Behr,
"The Artful Eater," 1992

3. To assemble and grill: Heat coals in a kettle-type grill. Skewer the vegetables, with each type on separate skewers. Reserve the vegetable marinade.

4. When coals are hot, grill the vegetables until just tender, removing first the ones that cook fastest. When cooked, return vegetables to their marinade and toss gently. Next, grill the beef to medium rare, about 4-5 minutes per side. (The chicken will take even less time.)

5. Optional step (do while meat is cooking): bring the meat marinade to a hard simmer in a small saucepan and reduce to a syrupy texture. Cool to warm or room temperature.

6. Let meat rest 5 minutes before slicing it at an angle across the grain. Toss the slices with the cooked meat marinade.

7. To serve: Portion the chopped lettuce on 4 plates; place meat and vegetables on the lettuce. Use some of the excess vegetable marinade to drizzle on the salads. Serve with freshly ground black pepper.

Tomsum—A Hmong Salad
4 servings

Here's a popular Hmong recipe from Kathy Khamphouy, who came to Madison thirteen years ago from Laos and works for United Refugee Services. She and her colleague, Xai Voung, often prepare tomsum for their co-workers at staff meetings.

Typically, tomsum is made with unripe (green) papaya, but carrots, cucumbers or even turnips make an authentic substitute. A sort of Hmong "cole slaw," it's served at room temperature as a spicy accompaniment to sticky rice or grilled chicken. To be genuine, it should be intensely spicy. As Xai says, "Every time we eat, we must have something hot, or we cannot eat!"

Note: Thai peppers are available at many farmers' markets. Or you can find them, along with dried shrimp and bottled fish sauce, at oriental food stores.

5-6 cups peeled and shredded carrot, cucumber, turnip or unripe papaya
2 teaspoons minced garlic
2-5 chopped red or green Thai chili peppers (two will make it very hot, five will light you on fire!)
½ cup roasted, lightly salted peanuts, ground
2 tablespoons dried shrimp, ground
3-4 thin slices tomato
3 thin slices fresh lime, plus additional lime juice to taste
2 teaspoons bottled Thai fish sauce ("nam pla")
2 teaspoons sugar (or more to taste)

1. In a large bowl or wooden mortar, combine 2 cups shredded vegetable of your choice with garlic and peppers. With a wooden pestle or large, sturdy spoon, smash and press until garlic and peppers are somewhat mashed. This will take several minutes; you'll be able to "hear" the moisture in the dish after a while.
2. Add remaining ingredients, along with the remaining shredded vegetable. Continue to smash and press mixture against the sides and bottom of bowl for 5-10 minutes, until vegetables are limp and juicy and ingredients are well combined. Add more sugar or lime juice to taste. Serve at room temperature.

Kathy Khamphouy
Madison, Wisconsin

A HMONG HERITAGE

The growing number of Hmong immigrants in Wisconsin has resulted in a new influence at farmers' markets in some of the state's larger towns. The Hmong are originally from the mountains of China, but migrated over a hundred years ago to southeast Asia; many came in recent years to America as refugees from the Vietnam War. When theirs was primarily a farming culture, the Hmong sold their produce and crafts at city markets. Today, that heritage lives on at markets in Wisconsin towns such as Eau Claire, La Crosse, Madison, Milwaukee and Green Bay. Typical midwestern vegetables are available at Hmong stands, along with special foods used in Hmong cooking, including these:

Pak choi—Also called bok choy, this is a kind of oriental celery. The stalk is bright white and retains its crispness when cooked; the leaves are deep green and reminiscent of spinach or chard.

Bitter melon—Looks like a pale-green cucumber with bumpy skin. The flesh is bitter and is usually cooked like zucchini, or marinated with cucumber in a tart, vinegar-and-onion dressing.

Thai peppers—Small, thin, green or red fresh chilies. Very hot!

Cilantro—Also known as Chinese parsley, cilantro is actually the young leaves of the coriander plant. It should be used fresh and is not to be confused with dried coriander seeds, which have a different taste altogether. Use cilantro sparingly, as it has a pungent and more distinctive taste than American parsley. It's used extensively in oriental and Latin American cooking.

Chinese cabbage—Eaten raw or stir-fried, Chinese cabbage has a long shape, white ribs and light green, wrinkly leaves. The flavor is mild.

Ratatouille Casserole
4 servings

Basic, versatile, nourishing, but best of all, delicious, ratatouille can be eaten alone or on pasta, in omelettes, as a sauce for fish and in many other ways. Mrs. Lorraine Mosher from Lake Mills bakes it with nutritious brown rice and a warm, gooey layer of Mozzarella cheese. You can double, triple, even quadruple the recipe and freeze the extras. If you like a spicy touch, add some red pepper flakes along with the herbs.

Ratatouille:

2 tablespoons oil (vegetable, canola or olive)
1 ½ cups chopped onions
3 cups cubed eggplant
2 teaspoons minced garlic
1 cup cubed zucchini
1 cup chopped green pepper
2 tablespoons chopped fresh parsley
2 tablespoons chopped fresh basil OR 4 teaspoons dried basil
1 ½-2 cups coarsely chopped tomatoes
Salt and freshly ground black pepper

Other Ingredients:

1 ½ cups cooked brown rice
1 ½ cups grated low-fat Mozzarella cheese
Additional chopped fresh herbs (for garnish)

1. To make ratatouille: Heat oil in a large, heavy pot and add onions, eggplant and garlic. Sauté until very lightly browned. Add zucchini, green pepper, parsley, and if you're using dried basil and thyme, add them at this time, also. Cover and cook over medium low heat about 20 minutes, stirring occasionally.
2. Add tomatoes, plus salt and pepper to taste. If you're using fresh basil and thyme, add them now. Cook 10-15 minutes, uncovered, until flavors have blended and sauce has thickened. Ratatouille can be refrigerated until ready to bake.
3. To make casserole: Heat oven to 350 degrees. Oil a baking dish. Mix ratatouille with brown rice, spoon it into the dish and bake until hot, 30-40 minutes. Sprinkle with cheese and bake until bubbly. Sprinkle additional chopped fresh herbs on each serving.

Mrs. Lorraine Mosher
Lake Mills Farmers' Market

Chicken Booyah
3-4 gallons—a crowd-size recipe

Booyah is a specialty from northeast Wisconsin, a "hand-me-down" recipe little known outside the Green Bay area. Special thanks to my sister, Judy Ullmer, for helping me get the elusive secrets of this well-loved chicken soup down on paper. You can vary the ingredients, but of course I think Judy's recipe is the *real* thing.

This recipe is dedicated to the memory of my dad, Norbert J. Allen, who was "one hundred percent Belgian," as he used to proudly say, and a true booyah connoisseur.

1 pound beef stew meat, in 1 piece
2 pounds onions, chopped
Bay leaves, salt and pepper
1 large stewing chicken (6 pounds), cut into pieces
1 bunch celery, chopped
1 pound carrots, chopped
1 pound cabbage, shredded
½ pound green beans, chopped
1 can (28 ounces) chopped tomatoes (or use fresh)
½ pound corn (off the cob)
½ pound peas (out of the pod)
2 pounds red potatoes, chopped
Juice of 2 lemons
1 tablespoon (or more) soy sauce
Additional salt and pepper to taste
2-4 beef bouillon cubes (optional)
Oyster crackers

1. Place the beef in a very large pot with some of the onion, a few bay leaves and some salt and pepper. Add enough cold water to fill the pot ⅓ full. Bring to simmer, skim surface as needed and cook ½ hour. Add chicken, more water (to keep meat covered) and a little more salt. Continue to simmer another hour or so.
2. Meanwhile, prepare all the vegetables as indicated.
3. When meats are tender, lift them out of the broth. While meat is cooling, add the prepared vegetables, including the remaining onion.
4. Remove bones and skin from cooled beef and chicken. Chop meats and add to pot. Simmer at least two hours—longer preferred. Water may be added during the cooking process, if necessary.
5. Season with lemon juice, soy sauce, salt and pepper and beef bouillon. Serve with oyster crackers.

Judy Ullmer
Green Bay, Wisconsin

BELGIUM IN WISCONSIN

Booyah is a heartwarming, tradition-laden chicken-vegetable soup that's a popular Belgian specialty in and around Green Bay, Wisconsin. You'll find booyah in few cookbooks, for it's one of those unique local recipes whose unwritten secrets are passed along through the generations. Individual cooks add their own touches, and fierce arguments are known to develop over the "right" way to do booyah.

Some aspects of making booyah are universal, however. Cabbage is a must, and you must include a variety of vegetables. Also, booyah must simmer a long while to develop the full flavor; thus, stewing chickens (not fryers) are preferred. Booyah is cooked in huge pots over outdoor wood-burning barrel-stoves; it's served at family reunions, neighborhood bars and church picnics. Everyone pitches in to help chop vegetables and provide taste-tests as the soup cooks all day. The large batches yield plenty of leftovers, which freeze well. Oyster crackers are the traditional garnish.

"Good thing we get company once in a while so we get something good to eat."

Norbert Allen

TWO WHO TEND HISTORY IN WEST ALLIS

The official title belongs to someone on a West Allis city commission, but many folks in town call Otto Bittmann the "Market Master." He's the guy who's been there every Saturday for the past 19 years, tending the market like a farmer tends his crops. Otto is the on-site manager at one of Wisconsin's oldest and largest farmers' markets, located in a handsome brick-and-stone structure in the heart of West Allis, near Milwaukee.

Otto springs from a creaky chair to greet vendors and customers entering his large, wood-panelled office. It's situated in the thick of the market flurry, with big windows overlooking the busy stalls. Here is where Otto deals with all that comes up when you mix 150 stalls-worth of farm fresh produce with thousands of bargain-hungry city shoppers. That could mean anything from giving directions to giving a vendor the boot for violating market regulations.

"Come in, come in! What can I do for you?" Otto welcomes the steady stream of visitors. Someone needs a phone. Produce advice. The frost report. Or simply a chair. (Otto offers his.) He's right there when you need him, and at no time is this more important than promptly at 1:00 p.m., when Otto pushes the buzzer to sound the official beginning of business.

At first, Otto wasn't interested in the job. He remembers: "I had just retired. I was travelling up north a lot. Then I said 'I think I'll try it afterall.'" Nineteen years later, "I'm still doing it. I love it!" The city of West Allis clearly loves him, too. In 1991, his birthday (July 6) was declared "Otto Bittmann Day."

But if Otto Bittmann is a longstanding, central figure at the West Allis Farmers' Market, then Lloyd Graser can be called an institution. After more than 60 years as a vendor, Lloyd not only knows the history of this market, he *is* the history.

Lloyd was a young boy when the town's first formalized market was set up over 75 years ago. The exchange of goods, however, was common as far back as 1835, when the area was known as Six Points and was a popular stopping place along the trade route to Milwaukee.

The West Allis market opened around 1917, according to Lloyd, who's happy to "sit for a bit" to talk about the old days. "But not too long!" cautions Lloyd with a grin. "Gotta get back to my stand."

Like the current market, the first official one in West Allis had a covered structure, but it was torn down when the land on which it stood was sold. "There was some question about whether or not there'd be a new market at all," says Lloyd. "Some of the farmers got together and went after some land in Milwaukee. To set up their *own* market." But the mayor of West Allis, Del Miller, knew better than to let them leave the area: the farmers' market was good for business, good for the town. "He said 'Wait!' " as Lloyd tells it. " 'We'll build you a new structure if you stay here.' "

Thus, in 1929, the new market was moved to its current location on 65th Street, and the city made good on its promise with a building in 1931. "That's when I got going," says Lloyd. "I can remember when corn was 15 cents a dozen. Raspberries were three pints for a quarter."

The West Allis market went through its lean years, especially in the late '60s and early '70s. In 1976, the market's location was threatened when a new police station was proposed for the site. After a lengthy town controversy, the proposal was dropped; the market stayed put and soon thrived again.

Lloyd and Otto have seen changes in their market over the years. Today, prices are higher; there's more variety, more and more people. Other than that, the West Allis Farmers' Market looks and feels much the same as it did 19—or even 60—years ago.

Even some of the faces are the same.

Fresh Market
W·I·S·C·O·N·S·I·N

FALL VEGETABLES

Winter Squash Soup with Corn and Kasha
4-6 servings

Just about the time the last of the corn is coming in at the market is when you begin to see the first winter squashes. (Can it really be that fall is on the way?!) Baking is the typical treatment for squash, but if it's still too early to turn on the oven, a creamy soup is a welcome idea.

Corn and squash, both indigenous to the Americas, have a natural affinity for one another. In this soup, chunks of squash are simmered in stock, then pureed; this makes a rich base for fresh corn kernels and kasha (buckwheat groats). Kasha, available at cooperatives or large grocery stores, adds substance and a chewy bite to this wholesome and unusually delicious soup.

Notes: If kasha is not available, substitute 2 cups cooked wild rice for the cooked grains. (To prepare wild rice, see page 135, and do not add the egg as described below.) Frozen corn can also be substituted for fresh. Homemade chicken stock is preferred, but if you use canned, reduce or eliminate the amount of salt called for in the recipe.

Kasha:

1 cup kasha
1 egg or 1 egg white, beaten lightly
2 cups chicken or vegetable stock
1 teaspoon butter or margarine
½ teaspoon salt

Other Ingredients:

1 tablespoon butter or margarine
1 cup finely chopped onion
1 teaspoon minced garlic
1½ - 2 pounds winter squash (acorn, butternut, etc.)
4 cups chicken or vegetable stock
2 cups (about 8 ounces) fresh or frozen corn kernels
½ teaspoon salt
⅛ teaspoon ground white pepper
2-4 tablespoons heavy cream (optional)
Chopped fresh parsley

BASICS IN BRIEF: HOMEMADE STOCK

To prepare chicken stock, start with two to four quarts of chicken bones and chicken scraps, preferably raw ones. Cover with cold water in a large pot. Add to the pot a couple of carrots, a large, halved onion (skin on), two or three stalks of celery cut into chunks, and a handful of fresh parsley sprigs. Sprinkle in several whole peppercorns and a teaspoon or two of dried thyme and rosemary (or other dried herbs). Bring to a simmer and skim. Continue to simmer over low heat 3-4 hours. Strain stock through cheesecloth or a fine-mesh strainer.

Chill overnight— uncovered or partially covered—then remove and discard fat layer that has risen to the top. A good, potent stock will be gelatinous when chilled. It can be used as is or intensified by additional simmering. Freeze unused stock in small containers. Use it to give flavor and richness to soups and sauces, to replace water when cooking grains or stews, or in many other preparations.

For vegetable stock, follow the same method, but substitute any of the following vegetables or vegetable scraps for the chicken bones: onions, leeks, carrots, celery, potatoes (and potato skins). Even mild-flavored vegetables like beans or corn could be used to make stock, but avoid the ones that develop a strong odor or taste as they cook (such as broccoli, cabbage, bell peppers). Vegetable stocks should simmer about one hour. Since there is no fat in vegetables, you won't need to chill the stock overnight to remove the fat layer.

1. To cook kasha: Select a skillet with a tight-fitting lid. Stir kasha and egg in skillet until every kernel is coated. Cook over medium heat (uncovered), stirring constantly, until each grain is separate and looks dry. Add two cups stock, 1 teaspoon butter or margarine and salt. Bring to a boil, reduce to a simmer, cover and cook over low heat until tender, 35-45 minutes.

2. To make soup: Melt 1 tablespoon butter or margarine in a medium pot. Add onion and garlic; cover and cook over very low heat until onions are tender, about 15 minutes.

3. Meanwhile, cut open squash and remove seeds. Peel squash with a thin-bladed knife. Cut squash meat into small chunks.

4. When onions are tender, add squash chunks and 4 cups stock to the pot. Bring to a strong simmer, cover and cook until squash is very tender, about 20-25 minutes. Puree the squash with some of the hot liquid in a blender or food processor.

5. Re-combine the pureed squash and all the hot liquid in the pot; add corn, salt, white pepper and cooked kasha. Simmer a few minutes until corn is tender. To enrich the soup, you may stir in 2-4 tablespoons heavy cream. Adjust seasonings. Serve each bowl sprinkled with parsley.

Autumn Food Fair Chili
12 or more servings

Not what you'd call a typical chili, this soup/stew of beans, grains, fresh vegetables and picante sauce is healthy and hearty. It's served at harvest time each year at Bright Eye Farm Market near Jacksonport in Door County, during their Autumn Food Fair. The market features organically grown vegetables from Bright Eye Farm as well as packaged and bulk natural foods.

The list of ingredients for Autumn Food Fair Chili looks long, but any beans or grains or vegetables may be substituted where desired. For example, if you don't have wheat berries, increase the amount of brown rice or replace it with soybean nuggets. No celery? Try

(continued on next page)

Autumn Food Fair Chili *(continued)*

mushrooms instead. Black beans, navy beans or black-eyed peas could stand in for any of the beans listed. Despite the variety of ingredients, this chili is very easy to put together, and it makes enough for a crowd, with leftovers for freezing.

1 cup garbanzo beans
1 cup lentils
1 cup red kidney beans
1 cup wheat berries
½ cup whole barley
½ cup brown rice
10 fresh tomatoes, chopped OR 4 cups stewed tomatoes or tomato sauce
2-3 cups chopped zucchini
1 ½ cups chopped celery
1 cup chopped green pepper
1 cup chopped onion
1 ½ tablespoons minced garlic
2 tablespoons chili powder
1 cup bottled picante sauce (or more to taste)
2 cups whole wheat pasta (elbows, twists, etc.)
⅔ cup chopped fresh parsley
⅔ cup chopped fresh basil
Salt

For garnish:

Grated Parmesan cheese
Corn chips

1. Combine beans, grains and seven quarts water in a very large, heavy soup pot. Bring to boil, then turn off heat, cover and let soak 1 hour.
2. Add tomatoes and cook over medium low heat 1-2 hours, until beans are tender.
3. Add next eight ingredients; simmer 20-30 minutes, until vegetables and pasta are tender. Add more water if the chili gets too thick.
4. Stir in the parsley, basil and salt to taste. Simmer another 5 minutes. You may also add more picante sauce if you'd like it spicier.
5. Serve each bowl with grated Parmesan cheese and corn chips.

Toni Christenson
Bright Eye Farm Market
Jacksonport, Wisconsin

"What constitutes an exciting, exotic ingredient is very much in the eye of the beholder and few things can be as compelling as fresh, locally grown materials that you know have been raised in a responsible way."

Alice Waters in her essay,
"The Farm-Restaurant
Connection"

CARRY ON

You don't have to limit your market buying to what can be loaded in your arms. An old fashioned, fold-up "granny" cart—the kind you can still find in some hardware stores—is just the thing for ferrying produce through the stands. It's especially handy during "heavy-veggie season," when potatoes, pumpkins and squash can wear you out fast.

Consider these other ways and means to tote your edibles: sturdy bags tied to the handle bar of a baby stroller (or use the stroller itself, if there's no baby in it!); a little red wagon; knapsacks, wicker baskets, or expandable net-bags; and saddle bags hitched to a bike—or harnessed to the family dog!

If you're in West Bend, check out the "Totes for Tips" program at the downtown farmers' market. Area youth clubs such as 4-H and the Girl Scouts send children each Saturday during peak season to help shoppers carry their purchases to their cars. The kids aren't paid, but they get to keep any tips they're given. Aren't your tired arms worth a quarter?

Bistro Leek Salad
4-6 servings

Bistro Leek Salad is full of vibrant tastes: lusty garlic and basil, sweet red pepper, pungent olives and marinated mushrooms. Serve only at room temperature, to bring out all the flavor.

Use young leeks for this salad—ones that are no more than 1½ inches thick. To clean leeks, cut them into ½-inch rounds, then rinse gently in a colander and drain well. If you don't want to prepare the marinated mushrooms, you may substitute fresh ones and sauté them with the leeks, but the flavor won't be quite as lively.

1½ **tablespoons olive oil**
2 **cups chopped leeks (use white and green parts)**
1 **teaspoon minced garlic**
1 **large red pepper, cut into bite-sized chunks**
½ **pound Italian Marinated Mushrooms (one-half the recipe on page 27)**
½ **cup Greek or kalamata olives**
1 **heaping tablespoon pesto (page 129) or chopped fresh basil**
Freshly ground black pepper

1. Heat oil in large skillet, add leeks and cook over medium heat 3-5 minutes, until they just begin to get tender.
2. Add garlic; cook one minute. Stir in pepper chunks and cook another minute.
3. Turn off heat; stir in mushrooms, olives and pesto or basil. Cool to room temperature and season to taste with freshly ground black pepper.

Spinach, Leek and Potato Soup with Shiitake Mushrooms
4-6 servings

Here's a good example of what can happen when you let the market inspire your menu-planning. I bought these ingredients one clear-blue fall morning simply because they looked so good: curly spinach, slender leeks, baby red potatoes and pale brown shiitake mushrooms. When it was time to plan dinner, it was as if the vegetables themselves told me what to make.

Note: Five cups of vegetable or chicken stock may replace the water and bouillon cubes in this recipe. Cultivated (white) mushrooms may replace the shiitakes.

3 slender leeks (about ¾ pound)
4 ounces fresh shiitake mushrooms
2 tablespoons olive oil
½ pound fresh spinach, cleaned, stems removed
2 salt-free vegetable bouillon cubes
½ pound small red potatoes, scrubbed
1 teaspoon fresh rosemary OR ¼ teaspoon dried rosemary
½ teaspoon salt
Freshly ground black pepper
Freshly grated Parmesan cheese

1. Slice leeks into ½ inch rounds and rinse well under running water. Lightly rinse mushrooms; remove and reserve stems. Cut mushroom tops into thin strips.
2. Heat oil in soup pot. Add leeks, mushroom stems and one quarter of the mushroom strips to the pot. Cover and cook over medium-low heat 20 minutes.
3. When leeks are tender, add 2 cups water and bring to a boil. Add spinach; cover and simmer 6 minutes. Blend this mixture in a food processor or blender until smooth. Return the puree to the pot.
4. Stir in the remaining 3 cups water and bouillon cubes and bring to a simmer. Cube the potatoes and add them to the pot. Stir in remaining mushroom strips, rosemary and salt. Bring to a simmer, partially cover and cook 20 minutes, stirring occasionally, until vegetables are tender. Season to taste with pepper and, if necessary, additional salt. Serve soup sprinkled with fresh Parmesan cheese.

GINSENG: ROOTS THAT GO DEEP

If morels are one of the priciest and oddest-looking edibles at Wisconsin farmers' markets, there's one item with an even stranger appearance, a higher price tag and a worldwide reputation. Ginseng, indigenous to Wisconsin, is coveted by peoples from around the globe.

Francisco Dremsa of San-Kor-Tea Medicinal Herbs, tends hidden patches of the precious root near Boscobel. He speaks of the powers of ginseng: "In Native American lore, there's something known as the 'doctrine of signatures.' This doctrine claims that foods which look like a certain part of the human body are, when con-sumed, beneficial to that part." Ginseng, a wild root sprouting a knobby "head" and longish "arms and legs," is the image of a person. So it is that ginseng is believed to be good for every part of the human body.

"It's recommended to eat ginseng after and between meals, for it aids digestion," explains Francisco. "Ginseng's good for your energy level; it helps build oxygen in the blood. Native Americans used it to keep warm. I think it's especially helpful to people who are run down and stressed out. There's even a myth that it's an aphrodisiac. Oriental

peoples use it as a regular tonic because ginseng works best over time."

Francisco has been harvesting the root since 1972, when a friend of his, an old man, revealed the location of his secret plot before he died.

While Francisco's ginseng thrives in the southwestern part of the state, it's father north, in Marathon County, that the greatest concentration of cultivated ginseng in the United States is grown. Hundreds of farmers invest considerable sums and a great deal of toil to reap the financial rewards of ginseng production: wholesale, it sells for up to $100 a pound, and is worth several times that when sold retail.

It's expensive, but a little goes a long way. Small pieces of ginseng can be steamed with fish or chicken, added to soups or chewed straight. The most common way to consume it, though, is by drinking it as a tea. Here's Francisco's recipe: "Steep about ⅛ teaspoon of dried, powdered ginseng (or use fresh leaves or root pieces) in hot water for 10 minutes. The flavor is very delicate. You can also combine it with mint in a tea."

Chocolate Zucchini Bread
Makes 2 loaves

Faced with the inevitable mountain of zucchini that sprouts from Wisconsin's rich soil, market vendors come up with the most ingenious recipes to promote this prolific vegetable. One of the recipes making the rounds in farm kitchens in recent years is Chocolate Zucchini Bread. You'll like it.

3 eggs
2 cups sugar
½ cup vegetable oil
½ cup applesauce or plain yogurt
2 ounces unsweetened baking chocolate, melted
1 teaspoon vanilla
2 cups peeled, grated zucchini
3 cups flour
1 teaspoon cinnamon
1 teaspoon baking soda
¼ teaspoon baking powder
¼ teaspoon salt
1 cup chocolate chips
1 cup chopped nuts

1. Preheat oven to 350 degrees. Grease two loaf pans.
2. With electric beaters, beat eggs, sugar, oil and applesauce or yogurt in a large bowl 1 minute. Stir in the melted chocolate and vanilla. Stir in zucchini.
3. Mix flour, cinnamon, baking soda, baking powder and salt in a separate bowl. Stir this into the egg mixture until just combined.
4. Stir in the chocolate chips and nuts. Pour into loaf pans and bake 1 hour, or until toothpick inserted in the center of bread comes out clean. Cool partially in the pans, then run a knife around the edges, remove bread and cool to room temperature. Serve as a snack or dessert (it's excellent drizzled with coffee liqueur or topped with ice cream).

Michelle Larson
Madison, Wisconsin

Marinated Brussels Sprouts and Red Peppers
4 servings

To show off the charm of Brussels sprouts, which are really miniature cabbages, halve them to expose the tiny layers inside, then marinate with sweet red peppers and Italian seasonings. You'll like the holiday look—bite-sized shapes in bright red and deep green—and the do-ahead ease of this dish. Serve Marinated Brussels Sprouts and Red Peppers on an hors d'oeuvres tray or as a cold-weather side salad.

1 pound Brussels sprouts (3-4 cups)
1 large or two medium red bell peppers (about ½ pound)
1 teaspoon minced garlic
¼ teaspoon salt
¼ cup olive oil
⅓ cup freshly squeezed lemon juice
1 bay leaf
1 teaspoon basil
1 teaspoon lemon thyme or thyme
¼ teaspoon ground black pepper

1. Pull off loose outer layer of Brussels sprouts and clip off protruding ends. Cut each in half lengthwise. Steam over boiling water (or cook in boiling water) 5-8 minutes, until barely tender. Rinse under cold water and drain thoroughly.
2. Meanwhile, cut red pepper(s) into bite-size triangles. Combine sprouts and peppers in a glass bowl or ceramic dish.
3. Mash garlic and salt to a paste. Combine in a saucepan with 1 cup water and remaining ingredients; bring to a boil, then pour over the vegetables. Toss gently and leave uncovered until cool. Marinate salad in or out of the refrigerator for one or more hours, stirring occasionally. The longer they marinate, the richer the flavor. Return to room temperature before serving.

X
MARKS THE SPOT

The simplest way to handle Brussels sprouts is to steam and serve them hot with a little butter and perhaps a squeeze of fresh lemon juice. Cutting a small "X" in the root end of each sprout before steaming cooks them quickly and evenly.

Fresh, young Brussels sprouts purchased at the market won't have any of the bitterness of the store-bought ones. Also, frost improves their flavor. Your best buy is a whole, sprout-studded stalk, though you may feel like you're carting an alien home!

ALL ABOUT KALE

It's surprising that more people don't know about kale. This dark green, leafy vegetable is chock full of vitamin A, remarkably easy to grow and very beautiful in the garden as a border or on the plate as a garnish. (Use it as a "bed" for salads, fresh fruits, etc.; it holds up better than lettuce or parsley.) Blanched, boiled or sautéed, it has a slightly piquant flavor that's distinctive, but not strong. Like Brussels sprouts, the flavor of kale improves with frost, so don't be afraid to buy it late in the season.

Dutch Oven Kale Dish
4-6 servings

In this lusty dish from Amy Van Ooyen of Iron County, cooked kale is mashed with potatoes and topped with chunks of sausage. Serve it with one of your favorite Wisconsin beers—go for a dark and foamy brew—and some coarse grain mustard. For a Scandinavian side dish, Amy recommends a sliced cucumber salad dressed with oil, vinegar and fresh parsley. Then, as Amy says, "Eet Smakelyk!" ("Eat with taste.")

1 pound kale
2 pounds potatoes
1 pound kielbasa (Polish sausage) or other smoked sausage
Salt and freshly ground black pepper
¼ cup breadcrumbs
1-2 tablespoons butter or margarine

1. Wash kale well and remove thickest ribs. Bring a large pot of salted water to boil, add kale, cover and cook over medium heat until tender (10 minutes). Drain, cool, chop and set aside.
2. Peel potatoes, dice and bring to boil in salted water. Cook 5 minutes. Prick sausages, add to potatoes and continue to cook until potatoes are tender. Remove sausages and set them aside.
3. Drain potatoes. Mash potatoes and kale together; season with salt and pepper to taste. Grease a casserole or Dutch oven, spread mashed vegetables inside and place sausages on top. Sprinkle with breadcrumbs and dot with butter or margarine. Can be held at this point until ready to bake.
4. To heat and serve: heat oven to 350 degrees. Bake casserole until heated through, about 30 minutes.

Amy Van Ooyen
Iron County Farmers' Market
Hurley, Wisconsin

REMOVE LABEL

CUT

Soda Bottle Sauerkraut
6 servings

Kraut is traditionally fermented in large, straight-sided ceramic crocks, the cabbage weighted by a plate-and-rock combination. David Eagan, a farmers' market enthusiast in Madison, has a unique, modern method for preparing sauerkraut, one that fits with both his penchant for recycling and the size of his household—small by old-time standards.

Though David uses the crock method for large batches, when he wants to make a smaller amount of kraut he ferments it in a clear plastic 2-liter soda bottle, one with the top section lopped off. "Soda bottles are made from PETE (polyethylene teraphthalate)," notes David, "a kind of plastic that is inert and impermeable to the high acidity of kraut. The transparent sides also let you see what's going on inside."

Sound like something from a school science fair? The method really is simple, and the taste is so good you'll never go back to canned kraut again. The recipe is easily doubled, tripled, etc.; use 1½ teaspoons canning salt per pound of shredded cabbage.

2 pounds thinly sliced or shredded cabbage
3 teaspoons non-iodized canning salt
A clean, clear plastic soda bottle, 2-liter size
A clean, one-quart Mason jar (or 32-ounce mayonnaise jar, label and glue removed), with lid, filled with water
Whole caraway seeds (this is my optional addition)

1. Cut off the top of the soda bottle where the sloping "shoulders" meet the straight sides. For bottles with a colored plastic cup base, slice off the sides of the cup, but leave the bottom attached.
2. Place cabbage and salt in a large bowl. Mix well. Let stand 10-15 minutes, until limp. Pack into the soda bottle, using the water-filled jar to press it down. Fill bottle with cabbage no higher than 2 inches below the rim. Place this contraption in a cool place (60-70 degrees), with the water-filled jar weighting the cabbage.
3. Press again a few times over several hours, until the liquid covers the cabbage. Note: Some cabbage is juicier than others; you may need to remove some of the water either now or throughout the fermentation

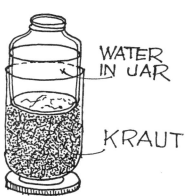

WATER IN JAR

KRAUT

SAUERKRAUT

A tradition since the German immigrants brought it to Wisconsin in the 1800s, sauerkraut is still one of the tastiest ways to enjoy cabbage. Sauerkraut is a low-calorie food that's also a good source of vitamin C. It's relatively high in sodium, but that can be reduced by rinsing it off. The ingredients and process for making kraut couldn't be simpler. All you need are green cabbage, canning salt and containers. (See recipe previous page.)

process. The liquid shouldn't overflow the bottle, but it must cover the cabbage in order for fermentation to take place. If additional water is needed, press cabbage until more liquid is extracted or remove a little of the cabbage.

4. The fermentation takes around 14 days. You'll notice a lot of bubbles within a day or two; they'll eventually subside. A scum or mold will form; don't let it bother you—simply remove it every other day or at the end of fermentation. Taste the sauerkraut occasionally, noting the transformation in acidity and flavor.

5. Sauerkraut can be eaten "raw" but most people simmer it first for 10-15 minutes. (For a wonderful flavor, add a sprinkling of caraway seeds when you cook the kraut.) The finished product may be canned (see page 64), frozen (some say the flavor improves after freezing), or refrigerated (where it will keep several weeks).

David Eagan
Madison, Wisconsin

Heaven and Earth
6-8 servings

Here's a variation of a German potato dish ("Himmel und Erde") that combines the fall flavors of freshly dug potatoes, tart apples, onion and—in this case—bratwurst. It's a great way to use up leftover grilled brats. Use the larger amount of sausage if the dish will be served as an entree.

Note: Serve with brown mustard, or stir a little directly into the dish along with the vinegar and sugar.

2 pounds red potatoes, scrubbed
1 pound tart apples (3 large or 5 small)
1-2 tablespoons vegetable oil
1 large onion, cut into ⅛-inch rings
½-1 pound cooked bratwurst, cut into rounds
1 ½ tablespoons cider vinegar
1 tablespoon sugar
Salt and freshly ground black pepper

1. Cut potatoes into 1-inch cubes. Combine with 1¼ cups salted water in pan or pot with tight-fitting lid. Cover and bring to boil. Meanwhile, peel, core and quarter the apples. Add to pan and cook over medium heat until potatoes are just tender, about 10-12 minutes (apples will have begun to disintegrate). Drain off most of the liquid. Keep warm.
2. Heat oil in large skillet, add onion rings and cook over medium heat for several minutes. Add bratwurst and continue to cook until onions are translucent and bratwurst is browned and heated through. Stir in vinegar and sugar.
3. Gently fold the two mixtures together, season to taste with salt and pepper. Serve hot or warm.

PRESERVATION PRECAUTION

"Canned apples are like gold in the bank—standard, and the person who refuses them is about as rare as the one who declines to eat good creamery butter. This canned material is not to be hoarded till next winter, but to be eaten next week, any meal when you are too busy to . . . cook."

Nellie Kedzie Jone's advice written to farm women around 1914 holds true today. Nothing beats the economy, nutrition and satisfaction of home canning, something that's sadly becoming a lost art in the wake of microwave ovens and irradiated foods. One of the best things about farmers' markets is that they allow even garden-less city folks to take advantage of the season's bounty and stock up for the winter ahead.

Canning can be fun, too, a lot more fun than another night glued to the television. But a word of caution here: whether you are a newcomer or a seasoned canner, you should be well informed about the possible dangers of home canning.

There are many books published about home canning; one that comes highly recommended is "Putting Food By," by Janet Greene, et al (look for the

latest edition). Your county is also a reliable source for the latest food preservation instructions. You can order publications on canning, freezing, drying and other forms of food preservation from the University of Wisconsin-Extension office in your county. You can also order publications or a catalog directly from the Agricultural Bulletin Office, Room 245, 30 North Murray St., Madison, WI 53715. The pamphlets cost only pennies, and that's well worth your peace of mind.

Broccoli and Apple Soup
4 servings

Broccoli is one vegetable that's available throughout most of Wisconsin's growing season. A wonderful way to give it a fall focus is by "souping it up" with tart apples. This recipe came from Eileen Madson of Sister Bay, via Dolores Allen's cookbook "Door County Recipes Old and New." If you're skeptical about the combination of broccoli and apples (as I was), you're going to be surprised at the tasty results.

3 tablespoons butter or margarine
1 large tart apple, peeled and chopped
1 cup chopped onion
3 cups chopped broccoli (peel the stalks first, and reserve a handful of the flowerets for garnish)
4 cups chicken stock, homemade (see recipe, page 54) or canned
Salt and freshly ground black pepper
Chopped fresh or frozen chives

1. Melt butter or margarine in pot. Add chopped apple and onion. Cook over medium-low heat until tender.
2. Add chopped broccoli and chicken stock to pot. Bring to simmer and cook, uncovered, until broccoli is very tender, about 8-10 minutes.
3. Strain soup, returning liquid to the pot. Puree solids in food processor or blender (add a little of the liquid if necessary). Stir into pot, reheat and season to taste with salt and pepper. Serve with a sprinkling of raw broccoli flowerets and chives in each bowl.

Eileen Madson
Sister Bay, Wisconsin

Nut-Crusted Winter Squash
4-6 servings

Stock up on plenty of winter squash at the end of the farmers' market season—select ones that have their stems intact, for they will keep longer. Most squash can be baked just like a potato—poke them two or three times and bake at 350 degrees until tender. Or cut them open, remove seeds and steam serving-size pieces over boiling water. Stuffed winter squash make a hearty cold weather supper (see page 136 for a wild rice stuffing recipe). Or try this Nut-Crusted Winter Squash for a festive side dish.

3 pounds winter squash (1 large butternut, 2 medium acorn, etc.)
½ tablespoon butter or margarine
1 tablespoon brown sugar
Salt and freshly ground black pepper

Topping:

¼ cup coarsely chopped nuts (hickory nuts, walnuts, pecans, etc.)
1 tablespoon brown sugar
1 tablespoon flour
1 tablespoon cold butter or margarine, cut into tiny bits

1. Halve squash; remove and discard seeds; cut squash into large chunks. Steam over boiling water in a covered pot (a steamer basket works great) until tender, about 25 minutes.
2. Cool a few minutes, then scrape squash meat from the skins into a bowl. Mash with ½ tablespoon butter or margarine, 1 tablespoon brown sugar, plus salt and pepper to taste. Grease a one-quart baking dish; spoon in the squash. Can be refrigerated at this point until ready to bake.
3. To make topping: Combine nuts, brown sugar and flour. Mix in the butter or margarine bits with your fingertips. Keep mixture refrigerated until ready to bake.
4. To bake: Set oven temperature to 350 degrees. Sprinkle nut topping over squash and bake 30-40 minutes, until heated through. Serve hot.

FOOD WISE

Author Wendell Berry has written that how we eat determines the very way the earth is used. In answering the question, "What can we do to eat responsibly?" he makes the following suggestions:

● Participate in food production to the extent that you can. Keep a garden. Compost your kitchen scraps and use it for fertilizer.

● Prepare your own food. Revive the arts of kitchen and household.

● Learn the origins of the food you buy and buy the food that is closest to your home.

● Whenever you can, deal directly with a local farmer, gardener or orchardist.

● Learn as much as you can about the economy and technology of industrial food production. Find out what is added to food that isn't food and what do you pay for these additives?

● Learn what is involved in the *best* farming and gardening.

From
Wendell Berry's essay,
"The Pleasures of Eating"

CONTINUING EDUCATION
Learning at the La Crosse Farmers' Market

School's over for most of us...but not at the farmers' market. There's no better place to continue your education, in a surprising variety of subjects.

Don't bother with chefs' schools or expensive cookbooks; you can get a culinary education directly from the people who know food the best—the ones who grow it. At a Saturday market in La Crosse, retired nurse-turned-grower Carol Pieper reels off creative ways to use her produce faster than a seasoned waiter recites a gourmet menu.

"These 'Jack Be Littles' can be filled with tiny pearl onions," she says, pointing to a pile of miniature pumpkins. "Or use the shells as individual soup bowls, for pumpkin soup!" She moves down the produce line, reciting ideas. Baked acorn squash halves can hold green beans drizzled with honey. Shredded daikon radishes dressed with lemon juice and olive oil make a stuffing for sweet red peppers. Multi-colored finger corn feeds the parakeet or amuses the cat. "And it's so much fun when you peel them," she says as she picks one up to demonstrate. "Each one is different, they're beautiful. You never know what to expect—you can get addicted!"

At the other end of La Crosse's double-rowed farmers' market, veteran vendor Nellie Pickle can tell you something of the history of the market, and how things have changed over the years. She's been selling her produce here since the La Crosse market opened in 1975. This is not the town's first market, however. Says Nellie: "I used to come to the old market, as a girl. I remember what it was like—I think that's why I wanted to be here when this one started."

Nellie enjoys giving economics lessons to her customers. "People ask me why prices are so high. They don't have any idea what goes into farming...the costs, the risks." She feels the farmers' market helps people understand and appreciate what they eat. It's a very basic, very important lesson. She's been known to offer agricultural "clinics" to area grade schoolers: "They come to learn how my peanuts grow."

She remembers one student who spied some of her tubers: " 'Those are sweet potatoes!' " Nellie quotes the surprised kid. " 'I thought they grew on bushes!' "

Carol chuckles about her own encounters with the inexperienced. Daikon radishes—huge, thick, white and hairy—trigger a lot of questions. One elderly lady asks if they are parsnips. A young couple guesses they are horseradish roots. Once, a fellow grower, thinking the giant radishes had perhaps mutated in his field, threw out his entire crop. Carol cheerfully sets the record straight in each case.

Nellie and Carol aren't the only teachers at the market. A gentleman who sells organic produce is happy to instruct you in its virtues, and to tell you about some of his offerings, typical in by-gone days, but exotic today. They include butternuts, elderberries and hickory nuts.

The fellow down the row who offers blue potatoes admits "I just wanted to be able to say I grow red, white and blue potatoes!" and informs you they cook up true blue, "as blue as these blue jeans." A woman standing nearby gives a short lecture to the clustering buyers about the

hundreds of potato varieties in South America.

The best lessons to be learned at the market may not be about food, or history, or agriculture, however. The best lessons are about how to be a good neighbor, about interdependence, about community. Carol helps a passerby find fresh basil because she doesn't sell it herself. Nellie expresses sorrow over a vendor who passed away—and concern for his widow. And all around is the knowledge that we're in this together—the growers and the buyers.

Fresh Market
W·I·S·C·O·N·S·I·N

BERRIES

Bea's Fresh Strawberry Pie
6-8 servings

This outstanding recipe comes from Bea Statz, of Statz's Berry Land near Baraboo. Bea and her husband Roman are true "strawberry people"—they own 10 acres of strawberries, selling them as pick-your-own or ready-picked. Roman is on the board of directors of the Wisconsin Berry Growers Association, and both Statzs serve their berries at events like the Sauk County Dairy Breakfast and the "Cows on the Concourse" celebration in Madison. Bea has compiled a cookbook called "Berry Good Recipes: Strawberry Recipes." She's also has been a judge at several berry recipe contests. Now, wouldn't you trust a strawberry pie recipe from folks like that?!

1 quart fresh strawberries
1 9-inch deep dish pie shell, baked and cooled (see side bar, page 16)
½ cup sugar
⅓ cup honey
⅛ teaspoon salt
3 tablespoons cornstarch
1 teaspoon butter

For topping:

1 cup chilled heavy or whipping cream
1 tablespoon powdered sugar
½ teaspoon vanilla
Whole strawberries for garnish

1. Rinse, pat dry and stem strawberries (but leave 6-8 berries unstemmed, for garnish). Arrange 2 cups stemmed berries, hulled side down, in pie shell.
2. To make filling: Mash the remaining stemmed berries in a saucepan. Stir in sugar, honey and salt. Heat slowly, stirring often, until mixture comes to a boil. Mix cornstarch with ¼ cup water, then stir slowly into the boiling strawberries. When thickened, remove from heat and stir in butter. Cool filling, then spread in pie shell. Chill thoroughly.
3. To make topping: Whip the cream with the powdered sugar and vanilla (see side bar). Spread over pie filling and garnish with whole berries.

Bea Statz
Statz's Berry Land
"Four miles north of Baraboo off U.S. Highway 12"

BASICS IN BRIEF: WHIPPED CREAM

- For reliability and best flavor, buy heavy or whipping cream and avoid ultrapasteurized cream.

- Use a copper, glass or stainless steel bowl; chill it and the beaters thoroughly before whipping the cream.

- The cream, too, must be well chilled. Make sure it's fresh!

- Pour the chilled cream into the chilled bowl and begin immediately to whip on high speed. The more air incorporated, the greater the volume of whipped cream, so move the beaters up, down and around while whipping.

- Add any sweeteners (sugar, honey, powdered sugar) and flavorings (vanilla extract, liqueurs, grated lemon peel) after the cream has taken shape, when soft peaks just begin to form. Some recipes call for unsweetened, unflavored whipped cream.

- Stop beating when stiff peaks form. Keep well chilled until ready to use.

BERRY FANS

Used as a garnish, whole berries will brighten up any plate. An easy professional touch with strawberries is to make narrow, even slices with a thin-bladed knife in the strawberry, going from just below the green top to the base of the berry. Then gently spread the sliced sections open a little and you'll have a pretty strawberry fan.

Chocolate-Gilded Strawberries
Makes enough to dip about 2 quarts of berries

Recipes don't get any easier or better than this. Serve these glorious dipped berries alone, with other dipped fruit, or as a garnish on a special occasion dessert. Just-ripe berries and high-quality chocolate make this simple recipe splendid.

8 ounces semisweet chocolate, cut into small chunks (can also use chocolate chips)
4 tablespoons butter
Fresh whole strawberries, stems on

Slowly melt chocolate and butter over simmering water. Stir until smooth. Turn off heat. Gently rinse berries and pat dry. Dip each one in the chocolate (leave some of the red showing) and place on waxed paper. Chill.

Yogurt Nut-Dipped Strawberries

Just as appealing as the previous recipe, Yogurt Nut-Dipped Strawberries make a more healthful dessert or snack. Simply rinse and pat dry fresh strawberries (stems on). Mound in a large bowl and display with two smaller bowls of vanilla yogurt and toasted, crushed almonds or chopped pistachios. Then it's "everybody-for-themselves" for some double dipping.

Strawberry Cream Cheese Torte
8 servings

Frozen, thawed berries work perfectly in this old-fashioned recipe for Strawberry Cream Cheese Torte. It's a welcome reminder of summer when winter gets wicked. Carol Schlei, of Mahn's Farm Market in Oak Creek, says the recipe came from a 1957 Milwaukee County Extension Homemakers' newsletter.

Crust:

1 ½ cups graham cracker crumbs
¼ cup sugar
4 tablespoons butter, melted

Filling:

1 package (8 ounces) cream cheese or Neufchatel, at room temperature
½ cup sugar
2 eggs
1 teaspoon vanilla

Topping:

3 cups frozen strawberries, thawed (will equal about 2 cups when thawed)
¼ cup sugar
2 tablespoons cornstarch
1 tablespoon fresh lemon juice

1. To make crust: Combine crust ingredients and press into bottom of an 8-inch square glass baking dish.
2. To make filling: Heat oven to 350 degrees. Cream the cream cheese or Neufchatel with electric beaters (or in a food processor). Add sugar, eggs and vanilla and continue mixing until smooth. Pour over crust and bake until set, 20-25 minutes (it may take longer if you've used Neufchatel, which is lower in fat and higher in moisture than cream cheese). Cool on a rack.
3. To make topping: Drain berries over a sauce pan to collect the juice. Stir sugar, cornstarch and lemon juice into the strawberry juice. Cook over medium heat, stirring often, until thickened. Remove from heat, stir in drained berries and let cool. Spread over filling and chill thoroughly.

Carol Schlei
Mahn's Farm Market
Oak Creek, Wisconsin

IT'S THE BERRIES

Is there anything more welcome than berry season? Store-bought berries are absolutely nothing like the luscious, sweet, soft, juicy ones you can find at the farmers' market. For dead-ripe freshness, Wisconsinites also have their choice at many pick-your-own fields and roadside stands.

Try to use berries soon after you bring them home. They taste best at room temperature, but if you must keep them longer than a day, refrigerate them. Never wash berries or remove their green caps until just before using, and when you do wash them, be gentle—use a cool sprinkle of water. Allow berries to air-dry, or pat dry with a cotton towel.

Berry season is all too short, but as luck would have it, freezing berries is a very easy way to transplant the taste of summer to the chilly winter months. Remove stems, gently rinse and dry carefully, then pack into freezer bags and seal tightly. (Alternately, you may freeze the berries in a single layer on baking sheets, then package and return to freezer.) Thawed, they will be soft and much juicier,

but all the sensational summer flavor will be intact. A good way to use frozen, thawed berries in the winter months is to puree and add them to orange juice. What a great breakfast juice that makes!

Berries are a good source of fiber and, if served plain, are very low in calories.

BETTER BISCUITS

For topnotch biscuits, short cake or scones, follow these guidelines:

• Use fresh baking powder. To make sure it gets evenly distributed through the flour, you can opt to sift twice.

• Add only as much liquid as is needed to hold the dough together.

• Don't overwork the dough: knead lightly and briefly.

• Roll or pat dough at least 1 inch thick. When cutting, don't twist or turn the blade or you'll seal the edges and prevent a high rise.

• Place biscuits ½ inch apart in an ungreased pan, or, if you prefer crispy edges, place them farther apart.

• Use a very hot oven (450 degrees).

Berry Lemon Short Cake
6-8 servings

Homemade short cake makes the very best bottom for these little stacks of heaven. Any fresh or thawed berries—raspberries, strawberries, blackberries, blueberries, mulberries—may be used. And a small heap of whipped cream is the classic finish.

Short Cake:

1¾ cups flour
2 tablespoons sugar
3 teaspoons baking powder
¼ teaspoon salt
3 tablespoons cold butter, cut into small pieces
1 teaspoon finely grated lemon peel
1 tablespoon lemon juice
Scant ¾ cup milk

Berry Topping:

2-3 pints fresh or thawed berries of any persuasion
Sugar to taste
2 tablespoons berry liqueur (optional)

Sweetened whipped cream (see side bar, page 70)

1. To make short cake: Preheat oven to 450 degrees. Sift flour, sugar, baking powder and salt in a bowl. Cut in butter until pieces are the size of sunflower seeds.
2. Sprinkle grated lemon peel over the mixture; make a well in the center. Combine lemon juice and milk; stir into flour mixture.
3. Turn dough onto a floured surface; knead briefly (3-4 turns). Roll or pat to a thickness of one inch.
4. Cut with a 3-inch biscuit cutter into rounds, or with a sharp knife into triangles. Place in ungreased pan. (Gather dough scraps and repeat, for a total of 6-8 cakes). Bake 13-14 minutes, until high and golden brown. Cool to slightly warm or room temperature.
5. Meanwhile, make berry topping: Combine ingredients, using only as much sugar as needed to bring out the natural sweetness of the berries. Let stand at room temperature until berries get "saucy," about 20-30 minutes.
6. To serve, split short cakes in half lengthwise. Serve "singles" or "doubles" with the berry topping ladled over and whipped cream on top.

Blackberry Grunt
6 servings

"Grunt" is the funny name given to a colonial dish of berries topped with sweet dumplings. It's a wonderful summer treat for it's prepared on top of the stove, not in the oven. It will, however, provide homey warmth for breakfast, brunch or dessert any time of the year.

This Blackberry Grunt has great berry flavor that's intensified by the addition of blackberry syrup, a special fruit syrup available at many farm markets like Jorn's Sugar Bush in Egg Harbor (see side bar). If blackberry syrup isn't available, substitute 2 tablespoons berry-flavored liqueur or brandy, increase water to 3 tablespoons and add ⅓ cup sugar to the berries.

The low-fat dumplings were inspired by a recipe by Richard Sax in a 1992 issue of Eating Well Magazine.

Note: Blackberries and blackberry syrup may be replaced with other berries and syrups.

Dumplings:

1 cup flour
3 tablespoons sugar
1 teaspoon baking powder
½ teaspoon baking soda
¼ teaspoon salt
½ cup low-fat milk
1 tablespoon melted butter
1 tablespoon vegetable oil
Cinnamon sugar to sprinkle on dumplings

Other Ingredients:

2 heaping cups blackberries
¼ cup blackberry syrup
1 tablespoon fresh lemon juice

1. Mix flour, sugar, baking powder, baking soda and salt in a medium bowl. In a separate bowl, combine milk, melted butter and oil. Stir the wet ingredients into the dry.
2. Combine blackberries, syrup, lemon juice and 1 tablespoon water in a medium skillet. Stir gently; cover and bring to a strong simmer.
3. Drop the dumpling batter by spoonfuls over the berries. Sprinkle lightly with cinnamon sugar. Cover skillet tightly and cook over medium-low heat 15 minutes, or until dumplings are firm. Serve warm.

SWEET THINGS

It's hard to imagine anything better on your Sunday pancakes or waffles than 100% pure maple syrup . . . but Steve Jorns did. Steve is from a long line of maple syrup producers in Door Country. He and his wife Dixie operate Dixie's Home-Style Preserves—making and selling homemade jams and their special fruit syrups.

Vividly colored in shades of red, gold and purple, Steve and Dixie's syrups line the shelves at the Door County Market and Bakery south of Fish Creek, and at many shops and farm stands throughout the Door peninsula. Cherry, apple, blackberry, blueberry, strawberry, bosenberry, crab apple and raspberry—each one yields intense flavor in a thick, clear syrup form.

Lengthy simmering, adding just the right amount of sugar and a clarification treatment are all part of the syrup-making process, according to Steve. Beyond that, he's not willing to give away any secrets. "It took a long time to get each one just right," says Steve protectively.

Steve and Dixie's syrups are worth the mystery. To get yours directly from the source, visit them at 4522 Highway T near Egg Harbor, or place a mail order by calling 414-868-3026.

BERRIES FROM HEAVEN

A bowl of fresh, ruby-red strawberries or raspberries topped with mounds of whipped cream will always bring out the "ahs." For another easy-but-exciting berry dish, sprinkle sugar and fruit-flavored liqueur over plump berries and let stand 15-20 minutes, gently stirring the mixture occasionally. Serve as is or over frozen yogurt for a low-fat dessert.

Other simple-but-splendid additions to fresh berries include:
• a sprinkling of vinegar (especially if it's balsamic vinegar) and sugar;
• chopped fresh mint;
• a drizzle of maple syrup;
• tiny bits of green onion and a turn of the pepper mill (yes, really!);
• a mixture of honey, yogurt and vanilla extract;
• a splash of port wine.

Try berries in your next tossed salad or drop a few into a glass of white wine or iced tea. Frozen berries can replace ice cubes in the blender for an outstanding batch of berry-based daiquiris. Toss bright red strawberries or raspberries with blueberries and a sprinkling of snowy white coconut for a Fourth-of-July breakfast.

Fresh Berry Smoothie
4 servings

Berry season brings out the smiles in Wisconsin. For a few beloved weeks we can get our fill of juicy, ripe raspberries, blueberries, strawberries—fresh-picked and eaten out-of-hand or included in one of our favorite recipes. People who plan ahead make the most of the short season and buy extra pints to freeze for the berry-less months we'll face all too soon.

Making smoothies is a delightful way to enjoy the happy flavor of fresh or frozen berries. Cool and soothing on steamy summer days, smoothies are also a comforting reminder of summer during chilly weather. Serve them for breakfast, as a snack or for dessert. With the help of a food processor or blender, delicious berry-based smoothies are only a moment away.

Feel free to vary the fruits and fruit juices used in this recipe. My personal favorite is a combination of tangerine juice and raspberries.

4 juicy tangerines, oranges or blood oranges
1 pint fresh (or frozen and partially thawed) raspberries, blueberries or strawberries
2 fully ripe bananas
2 tablespoons honey
1 tablespoon freshly squeezed lemon juice
½ cup milk, half-and-half or yogurt

Chilled club soda or citrus-flavored mineral water (optional)
Whole berries for garnish

1. Roll and lightly press tangerines or oranges against a work surface (to make them juicier.) Cut in half and juice them. Strain the juice into a food processor or blender. Add berries.
2. Peel bananas and cut into chunks. Add bananas and honey to work bowl. Process until smooth.
3. Add lemon juice and milk, half-and-half or yogurt. Process until well blended.
4. Smoothies may be served immediately or chilled thoroughly. To make a "smoothie-fizz," add club soda or mineral water to each glass. Garnish with whole berries.

Raspberry Ruby Sauce
Makes about 1 cup

Intense flavor and a drop-dead raspberry red color are the best features of this silky smooth and very easy-to-make dessert sauce. When raspberries are in season, double or triple the recipe and freeze some. The possibilities are many: spooned over ice cream; drizzled on cream puffs or pound cake; as a dipping sauce for fresh fruit; as a topping for pancakes or waffles; or stirred into warm oatmeal or cool yogurt.

1 pint fresh raspberries OR 1 package (10 ounces) frozen raspberries, thawed
4 tablespoons powdered sugar, sifted
2 tablespoons peach brandy or raspberry liqueur

Puree raspberries in a food processor or blender, then strain through a fine-mesh strainer. Use a spoon to press out every bit of the bright red liquid; discard seeds. Whisk in powdered sugar and liqueur. Serve chilled or at room temperature.

WISCONSIN CRANBERRY LORE

Customers have been purchasing cranberries at markets as far back as the development of the Northwest Territory, when Native Americans bartered or sold baskets of the wild berries to travellers and settlers. Native to Wisconsin, cranberries were one of the few fruits available in colonial times. Gathered from wild bogs and marshes, the tart fruit had several different names, but the title that has lasted is the one that was shortened from "crane berry"—a reference to the plant blossom's bird-like resemblance to a crane.

The growth of Wisconsin's cranberry industry began around 1860, when Edward Sadut of New York came to Berlin, Wisconsin to develop over 700 acres of bog that were rich with cranberry vines. His success led to the development of other marshes, and soon a cranberry boom was on. By 1894, however, cranberry production was way down in the Berlin area. Sensitive to frost, the cranberry bogs had fallen victim to several years of bad weather.

But the cranberry growers of Wisconsin didn't

give up. The center of the industry moved to the Cranmoor area, west of Wisconsin Rapids, and in subsequent years bogs were developed throughout counties in west-central and northern Wisconsin. Today, the cranberry is Wisconsin's No. 1 fruit crop and the industry is one of our oldest organized industries.

Happily, it's also one that has a particular concern for the environment. Cranberry marshes and the wetlands that surround them are close partners—the wetlands provide enough water to allow cranberry crops to thrive, while the bogs enrich and stabilize the wetlands environment in important ways. For every acre of cultivated cranberries, another 11 acres of support wetlands are maintained by growers. These lands provide a home to almost every species of wildlife in the state. Aldo Leopold, author of "A Sand County Almanac," credits the cranberry marshes—and their valuable, adjoining wetlands—with saving Wisconsin's sandhill crane from extinction.

Cranberry Cookies
Makes 3-3½ dozen cookies

Soft and chewy, with sweet dough and a fruity tang.

½ cup (1 stick) butter, softened
1½ cups sugar (divided)
¾ cup brown sugar
¼ cup milk
2 tablespoons orange juice or apple cider
1 egg (or two egg whites)
3 cups flour
1 teaspoon baking powder
¼ teaspoon baking soda
½ teaspoon salt
2½ cups fresh cranberries (about 8 ounces), coarsely chopped
1 cup chopped nuts

1. Preheat oven to 350 degrees. Grease cookie sheets.
2. Cream butter, 1 cup sugar and the brown sugar in a large bowl. Beat in milk, orange juice (or cider) and egg.
3. Combine flour, baking powder, baking soda, salt and remaining ½ cup sugar in a separate bowl. Mix in cranberries and nuts. Stir into butter/sugar mixture until just combined.
4. Drop by heaping spoonfuls onto cookie sheets. Bake 13-15 minutes. Watch the first sheet closely to determine the right amount of time for your oven. Cookies should be golden and chewy when cooled.

Michelle Larson
Madison, Wisconsin

Dried Cranberry Brown Rice Pilaf
6 servings

Delicious with duck or pork roast.

1 tablespoon butter or olive oil
1 ½ cups brown rice
3 cups chicken or vegetable stock (recipe on page 54)
½ cup craisins (dried cranberries)
1 teaspoon salt
½ cup chopped green onion
½ cup toasted, chopped walnuts or hickory nuts
Freshly ground black pepper

1. Melt butter (or heat oil) in heavy saucepan. Add rice and stir over medium heat for several minutes to toast it a little.
2. Stir in stock, cranberries and salt. Raise heat, bring to boil, then reduce to simmer. Cover tightly and cook over low heat 45 minutes, until moisture is absorbed. Turn off heat and let stand, covered, 5 minutes longer.
3. Stir in green onion, nuts and pepper to taste. Serve immediately.

THE CRANBERRY CAPITAL OF WISCONSIN

Warrens, a tiny burg in the heart of the cranberry bogs of central Wisconsin, doesn't have a weekly farmers' market, but it plays host each September to what might be the most incredible food festival in the state. Over 50,000 people swell the streets that are normally home to about 300 people, to celebrate an annual Cranberry Festival. Attractions include a gigantic antique/flea market, an arts and crafts show, parades, bog tours, cranberry videos, musical entertainment and contests galore.

To further celebrate the tart red fruit that made Warrens famous, food booths offer items like cranberry cream puffs, cranberry sundaes, and craisin (dried cranberry) cookies, plus a bewildering array of other Wisconsin specialties. A huge, temporary farmers' market offers fresh produce and features cranberries every which way: fresh, dried, juiced or jelled. An annual recipe contest yields creations like Turkey Tacos with Cranberry Sauce, Craisin-Stuffed Pork Loin, Cranberry Beef Stew and "Pink Lady" Salad Dressing.

How does a town so small manage an event of this magnitude?

"Well, it takes practice!" laughs June Potter, a Festival coordinator—a woman who remains uncannily calm in the midst of the wildness. "Everybody gets involved. They know their jobs." The Cranberry Festival celebrated its 20th anniversary in 1992, so the town has had plenty of practice.

Craisin Glaze for Steak (or Chicken, Pork, Turkey)
Makes about 1½ cups

Barbecue sauce recipes are usually carefully guarded by their creators; no one wants to give away their special secrets. Rochelle Schmidt was generous enough to share hers, and she won a prize for doing so. She entered her Craisin Glazed Steak in the Cranberry Festival Contest at the 1990 Cranberry Festival in Warrens, Wisconsin, and took first place.

Dried cranberries add a piquant difference to her barbecue sauce, excellent with any broiled or grilled meats.

½ cup craisins (dried cranberries)
½ cup coarsely chopped onion
1 tablespoon minced garlic
2 tablespoons brown sugar
½ teaspoon dry mustard
½ teaspoon ground black pepper
1 teaspoon liquid smoke
2 tablespoons vegetable oil
¾ cup bottled chili sauce

Combine first six ingredients in food processor or blender and blend until finely chopped. Add ½ cup water and remaining ingredients and process until well mixed. Transfer mixture to a small saucepan; simmer 10-12 minutes, stirring occasionally, until reduced and thickened. Use as a barbecue sauce for steaks, chicken, turkey or pork.

Rochelle Schmidt
Stevens Point, Wisconsin

Cranberry Cream Tart
8-12 servings

Warrens resident Shirley Johnson won a prize at the town's annual Cranberry Festival with the following extravagance. To cut calories and cholesterol, I lowered her amounts of butter and sugar, but this Cranberry Cream Tart remains a deliciously decadent dessert—sweet and creamy, rich, and gorgeous to behold.

Crust:

½ cup butter, softened
¼ cup sugar
1¼ cups flour
2 tablespoons milk
¼ teaspoon almond extract

Filling:

1 package (3 ounces) cream cheese or low-fat cream cheese, softened
⅓ cup powdered sugar
¼ teaspoon almond extract
½ cup heavy or whipping cream

Topping:

2 cups fresh (or frozen and thawed) cranberries, plus some additional berries for garnish
¾ cup sugar, divided
1 tablespoon cornstarch

Garnishes:

½ cup heavy or whipping cream
¼ teaspoon almond extract
1 tablespoon sugar
8-12 whole cranberries

1. To make crust: Preheat oven to 400 degrees. Grease a 9½-inch tart pan with removable bottom, or similarly sized pan. Beat softened butter and sugar in a bowl until light and fluffy. Stir in flour, milk and almond extract until well mixed. Press dough into bottom and sides of pan. Bake 12-15 minutes until light brown. Cool thoroughly.
2. To make filling: Combine cream cheese, powdered sugar and almond extract in a deep bowl. Beat until light and fluffy. Continue beating as you drizzle in the heavy cream. Chill filling thoroughly.

FOLLOW THE BOUNCING BALL

You've heard of the sniff test for melons and the snap test for beans, but how do you tell if a cranberry is fresh? It bounces! "At cranberry sorting stations, fresh market berries must prove their worth by bouncing over seven 4-inch barriers," write Mary E. Mennes and Nyla B. Musser in "Cranberries for All Seasons," a University of Wisconsin-Extension brochure.

Cranberries are sold in many ways: some are packaged fresh, but most are processed into sauces, juices and relishes. Dried cranberries are gaining popularity and make a delicious "native" substitute for raisins.

Fresh cranberries are easily frozen after purchase, so stock up at the farmers' market. They can be popped into your freezer without being washed or re-bagged. They'll keep 8-10 months and can be added directly to your recipes without being thawed.

The best news of all is that cranberries are nutritious—high in fiber and vitamin C, low in sodium, and not a speck of cholesterol.

3. To make topping: While filling is chilling, mix 2 cups cranberries, ½ cup sugar and ½ cup water in a saucepan. Bring to boil; cook 2 minutes. Combine remaining ¼ cup sugar and cornstarch; stir into cranberry mixture. Cook another minute or two until thickened. Cool and chill thoroughly.

4. To assemble: Spread cream cheese filling evenly over crust. Spoon cranberry topping over filling (to within 1 inch of filling edge). For garnish: whip cream with almond extract and sugar (see side bar, page 70). Decorate tart with dollops of whipped cream (a pastry bag works best) and accent each dollop with a whole cranberry. Chill and serve.

Shirley Johnson
Warrens, Wisconsin

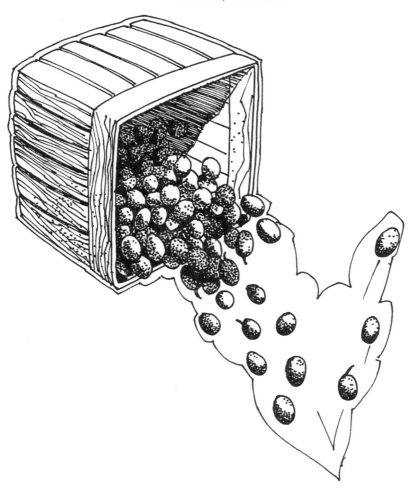

SOUL OF THE MARKET
John Sola and the Iron County Farmers' Market in Hurley

If just one word was allowed to describe John Sola, manager of the Iron County Farmers' Market in Hurley, it might be "character." A wiry, ruddy-cheeked senior citizen whose eyes shine from a deeply-lined face, John's speech jumps quickly from one point to the next and is scored with emphatic "okays" and "you-knows." In black jeans and well-worn running shoes, with wispy hair trying its darnedest to cover an impressive set of ears, John might be known, in some circles, as a bit of a character. But that's just a quick first impression, for the longer you talk with John, the more you think about the other meaning of the word character—as in, a man of character, of deep substance and commitment.

Like an old-fashioned preacher—not the fire-and-brimstone type, but the kind-hearted, good-deeds type, John is a spirited promoter of the market he helped start in Hurley ("where Highway 51 ends, and the fun begins!" as the brochures say.) In the late 1970s, John came out of retirement to join a committee formed to research and nurture agricultural development in their northern, recreation-based county. With a background in sales, John knew that the best way to encourage farming was to provide growers with a market—a farmers' market, in this case.

Tested first as a 4-H project, Hurley's farmers' market grew into one of the healthiest markets in the state. "Okay! Our producers now produce specifically for the market," boasts John. "It's where the city meets the country, every week, you know. People come rain or shine, 'cause it's something special."

One of the few markets in northern Wisconsin, Hurley's is also distinguished by having a pavilion, a roof structure that protects vendors and buyers during bad weather. With a black-topped pavement and sturdy wooden tables, the building is convenient for sellers, who can back their trucks right up to the stalls and easily display their wares.

What's remarkable is that the Hurley market happens through an unusual amount of community cooperation. Iron County provides the land, rent- and tax-free to the market. The pavilion and all its features became a reality through business, community and individual donations. Furthermore, the market is operated on a volunteer basis.

John Sola, who as manager does most of the operating, is clearly a driving force. Ever conscious of the value of marketing, John makes it his job to spread the good word. "I make sure we stay in the news," says John. "I go to every market. Keep a file of everything, you know." He stays in touch with the state Department of Agriculture and occasionally gets word of a fledging market in another town. "Helped one start up in Hayward, in '85, and worked with the people in Ladysmith, too." How much time does he put in on all this? "Quite a lot!"

It'd be difficult to find anyone more eagerly involved than John Sola in the direct marketing of Wisconsin farm products. He's rightfully known as the "father of farmers' markets in Iron County." I asked John why he thinks his market is so popular. "Okay," he ponders. "It's the mass displays, the color, the choice. It's the fresh produce and the fun." True enough, but it's also *you*, John. *Okay.*

Fresh Market
W·I·S·C·O·N·S·I·N

APPLES AND OTHER FRUITS

Rosy Applesauce
Makes about 3 quarts

When farm stands overflow with apples, it's almost impossible to pass them by, but what to do with that 10-pound bag you couldn't resist? Your intentions were good (visions of apple pies lining your windowsill), but a mild depression sets in when you realize you just don't have the time for pies or pastries. Well, when life gives you apples—too many, that is—just make applesauce.

Homemade applesauce is so much better than anything you can buy in a jar. Applesauce freezes well, so make a lot and save money in the months ahead. You can use your favorite type of cooking apple and adjust the sweetness to suit your taste. The addition of cranberries in this recipe gives the sauce a pleasing rosy red hue and extra zip.

5 pounds tart cooking apples (McIntosh, Cortland, etc.)
1 pound fresh (or frozen and thawed) cranberries
1 orange
4 cinnamon sticks (each 3 inches long)
1-2 cups sugar

1. Peel, core and quarter apples. Combine with cranberries and 3 cups water in large pot. Finely grate the orange (grate only the zest—the orange-colored part of the rind), then juice the orange. Add grated zest and orange juice to pot, along with cinnamon sticks and 1 cup sugar.
2. Cover pot, bring to a boil, reduce heat and simmer 30-40 minutes, until fruit is very tender. Add more sugar to reach desired sweetness, but don't overdo it. Mash fruit against sides of pot until smooth, or leave chunky. Remove cinnamon sticks. Serve warm, chilled or at room temperature.

"Comfort me with apples: for I am sick of love."

Song of Solomon,
The Bible

■ ■ ■ ■ ■ ■ ■ ■ ■ ■

BASICS IN BRIEF: POWDERED SUGAR ICING

For 1 cup icing, cream 2-4 tablespoons softened butter with 2 cups powdered sugar. Beat in 1 teaspoon vanilla (or other flavor extract) and just enough milk to bring the mixture to spreading consistency, about 3-4 tablespoons. Coffee, flavored liqueurs or cream may be substituted for the milk.

Amelia's Fresh Apple Cake
9 servings

Amelia Heal of Gays Mills developed this recipe from one in Country Woman magazine. She writes: "As an apple-grower's wife, I am constantly watching for new recipes for my customers. This recipe has the best flavor I have come across. The oatmeal and wheat germ are my own variations; I've also reduced the amounts of spice and still achieved excellent results. Black walnuts are great, if available."

You can serve Amelia's Fresh Apple Cake plain—as a coffeecake—or frosted for dessert. Amelia recommends a brown sugar icing, made by boiling brown sugar with a little cream and butter, then beating it with vanilla extract. Or use a powdered sugar frosting (see side bar). Frosted or not, you'll find the cake spicy, moist and wonderful.

2 cups peeled, chopped apples
1 cup sugar
1⅓ cups flour
1 teaspoon baking soda
½ teaspoon cinnamon
¼ teaspoon nutmeg
¼ teaspoon allspice
¼ teaspoon salt
⅓ cup quick-cooking oats
1 tablespoon wheat germ
½ cup vegetable oil
2 eggs, lightly beaten
½ cup raisins
½ cup chopped walnuts or black walnuts
Brown sugar icing or other icing (optional)

1. Preheat oven to 350 degrees. Grease and flour an 8-inch square baking pan. Combine apples and sugar in a large bowl; let stand 10 minutes.
2. Sift flour, baking soda, spices and salt in a separate bowl. Stir in oats and wheat germ.
3. Stir oil and eggs into apples, then add and stir in the flour mixture. Finally, stir in raisins and walnuts.
4. Pour batter into pan; bake 35-45 minutes or until toothpick inserted in the center comes out clean. Serve warm or at room temperature, frosted or not.

Amelia Heal
West Ridge Orchard
Gays Mills, Wisconsin

■ ■ ■ ■ ■ ■ ■ ■ ■ ■

Mahr's Apple Slices
12-16 servings

Here's an easy-going dessert that's as good—maybe better—than old fashioned apple pie. It's a kind of giant turnover, a mountain of sugared apple slices baked inside a flaky, golden crust, then frosted with a buttery powdered sugar glaze. No, it's not for the calorie-or fat-conscious. It's for apple gratification, pure and simple. Mahr's Apple Slices are wonderful as an after-school (or after-work) snack, as a dessert with ice cream, or as a brunch pastry.

Crust:

2 cups flour
1 cup vegetable shortening (preferably the butter-flavored variety)
1 egg
1 tablespoon cider vinegar
Milk

Filling:

2-2½ pounds apples (about 8-10; use McIntosh, Cortland, Melba's, Ida Reds, or your favorite)
½-1 cup sugar
2 tablespoons flour

Glaze Ingredients:

4 tablespoons butter, melted
1 cup powdered sugar
1 teaspoon vanilla
1-2 tablespoons milk

1. To make crust: Measure flour into a bowl. Cut in the shortening with a pastry cutter or with your fingers until the mixture just begins to hold together on its own. Lightly beat egg in a measuring cup; add the vinegar and enough milk to measure a scant ½ cup. Make a well in the flour, pour in the egg mixture, and stir with a fork until just combined. Dough will be a little wet. Refrigerate until ready to bake.
2. Preheat oven to 375 degrees.
3. To make filling: Peel apples and slice thinly. Mix with sugar and flour.
4. To assemble and bake: Place half the dough on a well-floured work surface and roll out to a sheet about 8 by 12 inches. If dough is sticky, sprinkle on additional

GAYS MILLS APPLE ORCHARDS

From a Wisconsin Historical Marker on Highway 171 overlooking the picturesque, rolling apple orchards of Gays Mills:

"Farmers in this area learned early that the land on both sides of the Kickapoo River offered excellent conditions for apple growing. In 1905, John Hays and Ben Twining collected apples from eight or ten farmers around Gays Mills for exhibit at the State Fair. The exhibit won first prize, then went on to capture first honors in a national apple show in New York. This experience prompted the Wisconsin State Horticultural Society to urge a project of "trial orchards" around the state to interest growers in commercial production. The Society examined a site on High Ridge and planted five acres with five recommended varieties. By 1911, the orchard had grown so vigorously that an organization was formed in Gays Mills to promote the selling of orchards. Today more than a thousand acres here produce apples nationally known for their color and flavor."

flour. Loosen dough from work surface with a knife or spatula, fold over and place on an 10 by 15-inch baking sheet with sides (for easier clean-up, the pan may be lined first with aluminum foil.) Unfold pastry. Mound apple slices over bottom crust, to within ½ inch of the edges. Roll out remaining dough, place over apples, and seal all edges. Bake 45 minutes. Let cool.

5. To make glaze: Whisk melted butter, powdered sugar and vanilla until smooth. Thin with a little milk. Frost pastry while it's still a bit warm.

Mrs. Henry Mahr
Mahr's Hillside Farm Orchard
Oak Creek, Wisconsin

Cashew Apple Salad
6-8 servings

Most "sweet" salads are just that—too sweet, but this one is wonderful. There's a hint of caramel apple in the flavor. Michelle Larson, who got this recipe from her mother-in-law, suggests using tart apples like McIntosh, and I recommend substituting yogurt for the whipped cream.

Dressing:

1 egg, lightly beaten
1 tablespoon flour
2 tablespoons white or cider vinegar
½ cup sugar (or less)
1 can (8 ounces) crushed pineapple, with juice

Other Ingredients:

4 cups unpeeled, chopped apples
1 cup whipped cream (see side bar, page 70) OR ¾ cup vanilla yogurt
1 cup cashews

1. To make dressing: Lightly beat egg in a small sauce pan. Whisk in flour. Stir in vinegar, sugar and pine-apple. Heat slowly, stirring often, until thickened. Chill.
2. To serve, mix dressing with remaining ingredients and serve immediately. (Cashews will soften if you let them sit in the salad too long.)

Michelle Larson
Madison, Wisconsin

Marion's Apple Oatmeal Bread
Makes 2 loaves

Bring some outdoor market goodness home and fill your house with the beloved smell of baking. Autumn apples, healthful oatmeal, graham crackers, brown sugar and cinnamon merge in this notably delicious quick bread. It's moist and sweet and freezes well.

1 cup all-vegetable shortening
1 cup sugar
1 cup brown sugar
4 eggs
2 heaping cups peeled, finely chopped tart apples
3 tablespoons milk
2 teaspoons vanilla
2 cups flour
1 cup graham cracker crumbs
1 cup quick-cooking oats
2 teaspoons baking powder
1 teaspoon salt
½ teaspoon cinnamon

1. Preheat oven to 325 degrees. Grease two loaf pans, each about 4 by 9 inches.
2. Cream shortening and sugars with electric beaters in a large bowl. Add eggs and beat well. Stir in apples, milk and vanilla.
3. Combine dry ingredients and stir into apple mixture until just combined. Spread in pans; bake 55-60 minutes, until toothpick inserted in center comes out clean. Cool on wire racks about 15 minutes, then loosen edges with a sharp knife and remove bread from pans to finish the cooling. The bread may sink a little in the center.

Marion Block
Madison, Wisconsin

DOOR COUNTY CHERRIES

If Wisconsin is known as America's Dairyland, then Door County, the "thumb" of Wisconsin that juts into Lake Michigan's west side, can lay claim to the title "Cherryland." The peninsula that's loved by vacationers year-round offers a special treat to summer visitors: buckets of plump, vivid-red, juicy cherries. Biking, sailing, swimming, golf—these are just ordinary means of recreation in Door County compared to the fun of cherry-picking in July. If you're heading that way when the cherries are ripe, bring a pail and join in.

Door County cherries are the tart type, the kind you pit with an old-fashioned hair pin and bake in a pie (though they're sweet enough to eat out-of-hand, too). If you're not the do-it-yourself type, you can purchase already-picked and pitted cherries, either fresh or frozen, at any of the dozens of cherry stands and farm markets that dot the Door County roadsides. Look for a Door County cherry stand at local farmers' markets throughout the state, too.

Cherry Snow
6 servings

Super-flavorful and simple to make, Cherry Snow makes a gorgeous, no-fat treat. Serve it in etched wine glasses either for dessert or as a between-courses refresher: *that* will make them sit up and notice.

If you'd like to keep this treat non-alcoholic, simply skip the wine or liqueur and increase the amount of orange juice.

¼ cup orange juice
¼ cup dry white wine or fruit-flavored liqueur
⅓ cup honey
3 cups pitted sour cherries, frozen

Blend orange juice, white wine and honey in a food processor or blender one minute. Add the frozen cherries, breaking them up somewhat. Using the pulse button, or an on-and-off action with the machine, chop the cherries until they are nearly pureed. You'll need to scrape the inside of the work bowl or blender occasionally. Cherry Snow is ready when it becomes a thick, frozen slush. Can be served immediately or kept frozen (let soften somewhat before serving).

The Wisconsin Cookie
Makes about 3 dozen cookies

Here's a goodie that would make a delightful Valentine's gift—one you might pack into the kids' lunch bags or stack in a pretty red box for your favorite aunt. Rich with the flavor of three Wisconsin ingredients—dried cherries, maple syrup and butter, this cookie was created by Margaret Guthrie, a Madison writer who also sells goat cheese for Fantome Farm of Ridgeway at the Dane County Farmers' Market.

4 ounces (1 stick) butter, softened
¾ cup packed brown sugar
1 egg, lightly beaten
¼ cup pure maple syrup
1 teaspoon vanilla
1 cup quick-cooking oats
1½ cups flour
½ teaspoon baking soda
¼ teaspoon salt
1 cup dried cherries
⅔ cup chopped walnuts

1. Preheat oven to 350 degrees. Lightly grease cookie sheets.
2. Cream butter and brown sugar in a large bowl. Stir in egg, maple syrup and vanilla. Combine oats, flour, baking soda and salt, then stir into butter mixture. Stir in cherries and walnuts until just combined.
3. Drop by spoonfuls onto baking sheets. Bake 10-12 minutes on middle and top racks of oven. Do not overcook. Cookies should be golden brown around the edges. Remove and cool on wire racks.

Margaret Guthrie
Madison, Wisconsin

SCENES FROM THE MARKET:
Door County

Highways 42 and 57 are the two main veins pumping tourist-blood through the "thumb" of Wisconsin's Door County peninsula, but there's no fast-lane living along these routes. Travellers must cruise a little slower if they want to enjoy the area's quaint lakeside towns, rolling orchards and sparkling waters.

If the views don't make you pull over and stop, the roadside markets will. They dot the routes in Door County like freckles on a smiling face, offering cherries, apples, smoked fish, and much more:

• A giant cherry tree painted inside the garage beckons visitors to the Richmonds' farm market, where apples from the family orchard play a starring role alongside a variety of other Door County products. It's picking season and the owners are too busy to tend the market themselves, so Grandma and Granddaughter have taken over. Do they have any favorite recipes for this cookbook? "Why, we just *made* some fruit pizza!" is the response. But what is fruit pizza? Grandma is off to the kitchen to fetch a tart spread with sweetened cream cheese and mounded with fresh blueberries and raspberries. Meanwhile, her grand-daughter provides entertainment by spelling Mississippi and the ABC's—backwards.

• The woman behind the counter at Hy-line, just north of Egg Harbor, has cheeks as red as the cherries she sells. If she looks exhausted, that must be because it's been a blaster weekend for tourists, right? "It's not the tourists, it's the cherries," she answers with a wan grin. She means the cherry-picking, of course.

• "What, no cheese? You gotta have cheese with your smoked fish!" This from the clerk at Koepsel's Farm Market in Bailey's Harbor. He thrusts a sample of 4-year-old Cheddar over the dairy case. "This'll melt in your mouth." So it does—and a half-pound chunk is added to the shopping basket that already holds a jar of pickled onions, some smoked whitefish, a six-pack of cherry beer, and a loaf of fresh bread.

Dried Cherry Scones
Makes 10 three-inch scones

Dried cherries have an intense sweet-tart flavor that's a delicious surprise to the uninitiated. Use dried cherries in the same ways you do raisins—in cookies, warm or cold cereals, in salads, over ice cream, or straight. Or try them in these Dried Cherry Scones.

Sweeter and a little more substantial than biscuits, scones are great during breakfast, brunch or teatime. See page 73 for helpful hints about baking scones.

Heaping ½ cup dried cherries
3½ cups flour, plus a little extra to sprinkle on cherries
½ cup sugar
1 tablespoon baking powder
½ teaspoon salt
4 tablespoons cold butter, cut into small pieces
2 eggs
½ cup milk or half-and-half
2 tablespoons cherry liqueur (optional)
½ teaspoon vanilla

1. Preheat oven to 350 degrees. Grease a baking pan.
2. Sprinkle a little flour over the dried cherries and chop coarsely. Combine with 3½ cups flour, the sugar, baking powder and salt. Cut in butter until the size of sunflower seeds.
3. Combine eggs, milk, cherry liqueur (optional) and vanilla; stir into flour mixture until just combined.
4. Turn onto floured surface and knead gently 3-4 turns. Press or roll dough to a thickness of 1½ inches. Do not overwork.
5. Cut into 3-inch rounds with a biscuit cutter, or into triangles with a sharp knife. Place on pan; bake 20 minutes. Serve warm or at room tempertuare. Freeze leftovers as they dry out quickly.

Wisconsin Fresh Fruit Crumble
12-16 servings

Friends are usually more than willing to be guinea pigs when it's recipe-testing time at my house. One night, however, one of them was very careful to explain how much he despised rhubarb. He warned me he wouldn't like this Fresh Fruit Crumble, tested with rhubarb frozen from the previous summer's market.

He ate two big helpings. And took some home.

I'm glad I didn't test it with apples or cherries, which he says he *does* enjoy. There may not have been any left for the other guests.

Note: If you use thawed rhubarb or cherries, you may need to thicken the juices with cornstarch or arrowroot in a sauce pan over medium heat before proceeding.

6 cups fruit: peeled, sliced apples or pears; chopped rhubarb; pitted tart cherries; cranberries; or a combination of two of these
1 cup white sugar
1 cup flour
½ cup dark brown sugar
1 teaspoon cinnamon
¼ pound (1 stick) cold butter, in small pieces

1. Preheat oven to 350 degrees. Spread fruit over bottom of a 9 by 13-inch baking pan. Sprinkle white sugar evenly over the fruit.
2. Mix flour, brown sugar and cinnamon in a bowl. Cut in the butter with a pastry cutter until the size of tiny peas. Spread this mixture over fruit. Bake 45 minutes. Serve warm with vanilla ice cream.

Gail Zahn
Zahn's Green Thumb
Sturgeon Bay, Wisconsin

"As we arrive at the market, it's hard to know where to start. We first see bushel baskets filled with tomatoes, vine-ripened and full of flavor. At the next table, loose, tender heads of butter lettuce share space with cucumbers, red and white radishes, bunches of spring onions with the moist earth still clinging to them, garlic and shallots, and bouquets of fresh herbs sitting in pails of water. The effect is of a colorful seed catalog come to vibrant life."

Richard Sax
with Sandra Gluck,
"From The Farmers'
Market," 1986

Outrageous Rhubarb Coffee Cake
12-18 servings

This is one of those wickedly delicious recipes that's been passed down and around so much nobody knows where the original came from. It's super-moist and rich, but if you want to watch the fat content, use the smaller amount of melted butter or margarine, and halve the amount of the topping. It'll still be a knockout.

Note: Sliced strawberries or pitted tart cherries could be substituted for, or added to, the rhubarb.

1 cup buttermilk
¼-½ cup melted butter or margarine
1 egg
1 teaspoon vanilla
3 cups chopped rhubarb
2¾ cups flour
1 cup sugar
1 teaspoon baking soda
½ teaspoon salt
1 cup brown sugar
½ cup chopped nuts

Topping:

½ cup (8 tablespoons) butter
½ cup light cream, half-and-half or evaporated milk
1 cup sugar
1 teaspoon vanilla

1. Heat oven to 350 degrees. Grease a 9 by 13-inch baking pan.
2. Mix buttermilk, melted butter or margarine, egg and vanilla. Stir in rhubarb. In a separate bowl, mix flour, white sugar, baking soda and salt. Stir the wet ingredients into the dry until just combined.
3. Spread batter in pan; sprinkle brown sugar and nuts on top. Bake 45-55 minutes, until toothpick inserted in center of cake comes out clean.
4. Meanwhile, stir and heat the topping ingredients in a small saucepan. When coffee cake comes out of the oven, poke deep holes over the entire surface with a meat fork or skewer. Drizzle the warm sauce over the cake. Cool and serve.

Laura Cominetti
Arena, Wisconsin

Easy Rhubarb Sauce

Wisconsin's earliest-ripening fruit, rhubarb, is actually a vegetable. A prolific perennial better known in Wisconsin as "pie plant," its super-tart flavor is sweetened up in pies and preserves. The easiest way to enjoy rhubarb is as a sauce, like applesauce. It's so easy, it barely needs a recipe. Try it warm or cold, alone or as a topping for ice cream or waffles.

Fresh rhubarb
Honey or sugar
Cinnamon
Grated orange or lemon peel (optional)
Freshly ground black pepper

Wash and coarsely chop rhubarb stalks (discard the leaves—they are poisonous). Place in a saucepan. For each pound of rhubarb, add two tablespoons water, ½ cup honey or sugar, ½ teaspoon cinnamon, 1 teaspoon grated orange or lemon peel (optional) and a grinding of black pepper. Bring to a simmer and cook gently 15-20 minutes, until tender. Add more honey or sugar to suit your taste. For every pound of rhubarb, the recipe will yield 4-6 servings.

Cozy Pears
6 servings

Serve warm inside crepes, as a simple topping for buttermilk pancakes or as a dessert sauce over ice cream. Use a flavorful variety like Moonglow pears for this recipe.

3 pounds firm pears, just ripe
4 tablespoons butter
2 tablespoons sugar
1 teaspoon cinnamon
2 tablespoons pear liqueur (orange liqueur or brandy may
  be substituted)

Peel, core and slice pears ¼ inch thick. Melt butter in large skillet over medium heat. It will foam for a short while. Add the pears and sprinkle on the sugar and cinnamon. Cook gently, stirring occasionally, 3-4 minutes, until the pears are just tender. Stir in the liqueur and cook one minute longer. Let cool slightly; serve warm over pancakes or ice cream, roll into crepes or eat as is.

"In the market is life, vitality, health, abundance, grit, prime produce, color. In markets lie the thick of things, sociability, the throb of human community. They provide links with the past, and all indications suggest that farmers' market networks will create far-reaching and revolutionary changes in the ways we shop and eat—alterations that will affect the face of agriculture's future."

Judith Olney,
"The Farm Market
Cookbook," 1991

■ ■ ■ ■ ■ ■ ■ ■ ■ ■

"Friends are like melons. Shall I tell you why? To find one good you must a hundred try."

Claude Mermet, 1600

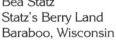

Summer Sunrise Melon and Spinach Salad
6-8 large servings

The bright, sunrise orange of canteloupe and leafy green of spinach make this salad beautiful, while bits of scallions and toasty sesame seeds make it delicious. Serve it in August, when melons are at their market peak. (Or substitute fresh strawberries earlier in the summer.)

1½ **pounds fresh spinach**
2 **tablespoons sesame seeds**
⅓ **cup red wine vinegar**
2 **tablespoons minced green onion**
1 **tablespoon sugar**
1 **teaspoon paprika**
½ **teaspoon Worcestershire sauce**
⅓ **cup vegetable oil**
2-3 **cups canteloupe chunks (or hulled strawberries)**
Freshly ground black pepper

1. Wash spinach. Tear into bite-size pieces, removing stems. Dry in a salad spinner or clean towel. Chill spinach.
2. Toast sesame seeds in a small, dry skillet over medium heat until golden, about 3-4 minutes. Do not scorch.
3. Mix vinegar, green onion, sugar, paprika and Worcestershire sauce in a bowl; whisk in oil in a thin stream.
4. Just before serving, toss spinach, sesame seeds, dressing and fruit in a large glass bowl. Pass the pepper mill.

Bea Statz
Statz's Berry Land
Baraboo, Wisconsin

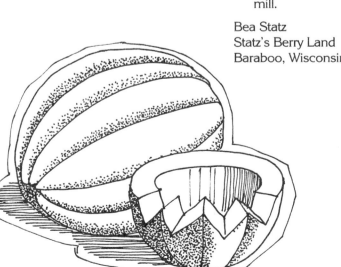

Suyapa's Fresh Fruit Punch
Makes 4-6 quarts

This makes a lot, but it's a simple process and the punch will go fast with young and old at a picnic or potluck. Feel free to vary the fruits—and their amounts.

1 small watermelon
1 pineapple
4 oranges
1 large canteloupe
2 large bananas
1 pint raspberries
1 pint blackberries
2 packages (each 0.13 ounce) unsweetened, raspberry-flavored soft drink mix
1½ cups sugar
Chilled lemon sour soda

1. Seed watermelon and finely dice about half of the flesh to make 3 cups. Puree the remaining watermelon "meat." Combine diced watermelon and the puree in a large jug.
2. Cut rind off pineapple, slice it in half lengthwise and cut out core. Finely dice enough of the pineapple to make 3 cups. Puree the remaining flesh. Add fruit and puree to watermelon mixture.
3. Slice off orange rinds, down to the flesh. Cut oranges open, remove seeds, then finely dice flesh and add to other fruit. Also, finely dice canteloupe and bananas and stir them in.
4. Puree raspberries and press through a sieve into the chopped fruit. Discard seeds. Repeat this with the blackberries.
5. Stir in packaged soft drink mix, sugar and 2 cups water. Let mixture stand, unrefrigerated, for 2 hours to develop flavor.
6. To serve, pour in 1-2 quarts soda (or you may add the soda by the glass). The full flavor comes out when the punch is served at room temperature, but it's also delicious chilled.

FROM HONDURAS WITH LOVE

The mountain-rimmed city of San Pedro Sula, Honduras may be an unlikely setting to inspire a recipe for a Wisconsin cookbook, but that's where I was when I first made the Fresh Fruit Punch on this page. On a trip to learn more about life in Central America, I once spent several days cooking for a day-care center in one of the city's poor suburbs.

On the first morning there, a group of us went to the city's open-air market to buy food for the week. Now, if you think Wisconsin farmers' markets are marvelous, you should see San Pedro's. It's almost impossible to believe the gigantic mounds of fresh produce, the displays of meats and fish and other foods—and to realize that most of the city's population can't afford to take advantage of this plenty.

We splurged, however, because the day-care was celebrating that week and a party was planned for all the children and their families. On the day of the event, under the direction of a gentle, doe-eyed cook named Suyapa, we prepared pounds of refried beans, spicy sausages and chopped vegetables, which

were later layered on warm tortillas. We also diced a mountain of juicy fruit to make Suyapa's special punch. Spiked with citrus soda and chunky with fresh fruit, it tasted as good as the morning sun feels.

The recipe on the previous page comes very close to the bright-flavored, thirst-quenching concoction from far-away Honduras, but only when you include some of the vine-ripened fruits from our own wonderful markets here in Wisconsin. And when you take the first sip, don't forget to toast Suyapa.

*"Summer's loud laugh
Of scarlet ice
A melon
slice"*

Jose Juan Tablada

Curried Shrimp with Melon Wedges
4 main-course servings, 6-8 as an appetizer

This exotic combination of sautéed shrimp, curry seasonings and fresh melon wedges can be served with rice or couscous as a main course, or alone as an appetizer.

¾ cup flour
3 teaspoons curry powder
2 teaspoons salt
½ teaspoon white pepper
½ teaspoon cumin
½ teaspoon cinnamon
½ teaspoon coriander
2 eggs or 3 egg whites
1 teaspoon turmeric
1 pound large shrimp
1 small canteloupe
1½ tablespoons olive oil
1½ teaspoons minced garlic
1 teaspoon grated fresh ginger root
1 tablespoon lemon juice
1-2 tablespoons chopped cilantro (fresh coriander)
1 cup plain, no-fat yogurt

1. Combine the first seven ingredients in a medium bowl. Whisk eggs and turmeric in a separate bowl.
2. Peel shrimp, but leave the tails on. Clean shrimp by running a sharp knife down the back of each to the tail, and removing the dark strip.
3. Cut melon (rind and seeds removed) into wedges about 3 inches in length.
4. Heat olive oil in large skillet (use two if necessary to avoid crowding the shrimp). Lightly toss shrimp in flour mixture. Shake off excess flour, then dip each shrimp in egg mixture and place in pan. Sprinkle garlic and ginger over shrimp. Cook over medium-high heat 3 minutes. Turn shrimp and continue to cook until just tender. Gently stir in melon wedges and lemon juice; heat through. Sprinkle with coriander. Serve with yogurt, either as a dipping sauce or dolloped on each serving.

DAYS OF APPLES PASSED:
Ela Orchard of Rochester

Ask Bob Willard to tell you about one of his apple varieties and you're likely to hear a discourse that's as descriptive and knowledgeable as a wine steward's. Bob and his cousin Edwin Ela grow over 30 varieties of apples and pears at Ela Orchard in Rochester, Wisconsin; theirs is the third generation to care for the orchard that's been in the family since the 1920s.

The Ela Orchard stand is one of the really busy ones at the Dane County Farmers' Market, with buyers four and five deep crowding close to the stacks of fruit-laden wood crates. Jugs of fresh cider—a blend of the current week's ripe apples— sit on a low table near by, but you've got to get to those early or they'll be gone.

Despite the crowd, you always get special attention from Bob. He nods, grinning a greeting at each customer, and seems delighted to answer the frantic stream of questions coming at him: "What are the best pie apples today?" "When will the Jonathans be ready?" "What does an Ida Red taste like?" "Got any pears left?"

Where other vendors give out carefully portioned tastes of their wares, Bob thrusts whole apples at you. Ask him how sweet the cider is this week and he'll pour you a glass himself. And when the little red arrow on the scale reaches the weight you requested, he figures the price of your apples, shrugs a "why not?" then tosses in a few more, on the house.

In a state that boasts hundreds of apple growers, Ela Orchard is recognized for both the quality and diversity of its products. Typical Wisconsin varieties are available—Lodi, McIntosh, Cortland, Wealthy, Red and Golden Delicious, Paula Reds, Melbas and more. Ela's is also one of the few businesses to offer heirloom varieties, those "born again" by cutting grafts from old trees at the orchard. These have charming names like Northern Spy, Wolf River, Tolman Sweet and Black Willow Twig.

One heirloom apple excellent for out-of-hand eating is the Golden Russett. It's "the last one to come in," says Bob. "Think of it as the Halloween apple." Golden Russetts have a pretty yellow color, with bronze speckles, crisp texture and a distinctive, almost pear-like flavor. Its origins are a mystery, and it's one of the oldest of the heirlooms.

"Snow Apples are another one of the old-time varieties," Bob notes. "Senior citizens really like the Snows. They remember the sweet flavor, their bright, white flesh and pretty red skin. And Snows have a nice tender bite that's easy on the teeth."

"One week at the market," he goes on, "there was one old gent who was really giving the Snows a going over. He wanted to be sure they were the ones he remembered from way back. Someone told him to go ahead and try one. He took a bite. His face lit up, and he said, 'By god, I'll take a quarter's worth!'"

Fresh Market

W·I·S·C·O·N·S·I·N

MEATS AND FISH

Apple Cider Pork Chops
2 servings

An apple cider glaze accents pork loin chops simply and beautifully. Serve them with fluffy baked potatoes and garden-fresh vegetables, and you've got a marvelous and characteristic Wisconsin meal. This recipe is easily doubled.

1-2 teaspoons butter
2 center-cut pork loin chops (each 8-10 ounces), about
   one inch thick
Salt and freshly ground black pepper
¼ cup chopped onion or 2 tablespoons minced shallots
⅔ cup apple cider
Chopped fresh parsley

1. In a skillet just large enough to fit the chops without crowding them, melt butter over medium high heat. When it begins to sizzle (but hasn't yet turned brown), add the chops to the pan. Brown on both sides.
2. Reduce heat, season chops with salt and pepper, cover and cook over low heat 5 minutes. Remove cover, turn chops and add onion (or shallots). Cover and cook another 5 minutes, or until just done. Do not overcook or pork will dry out.
3. Remove chops and keep warm. Raise heat, pour in cider, and simmer hard for a few minutes, scraping up bits from bottom of the pan, until syrupy. Pour glaze over pork chops, sprinkle with parsley and serve.

Mother King's Maple Glazed Pork Kebobs
4 servings

At first, Rick King, who sells his family's pure maple syrup at the Dane County Farmers' Market, denied that he had any recipes in his repertoire that would be "special" enough for this cookbook. I often visit his stand to chat, and I admit to a bit of badgering on my part. Turns out it's a good thing I persisted, for he finally gave me this recipe for Maple Glazed Pork Kebobs, and it's a winner. Lean pork, vegetable chunks and fresh

THIS LITTLE PIGGY WENT TO MARKET

If you've never thought of Wisconsin as a pork-producing state, think again. Our southwestern counties are worthy rivals to their more well known pig-raising neighbors in Iowa and Illinois. (It's been said that Wisconsin's Grant County has more pigs than people.) Sausage-making is a tradition in small butcher shops throughout the state, and a variety of sausages as well as many pork cuts are available at some of the state's farmers' markets.

Nationwide, pork is touted as "the other white meat," and while that may be stretching things a bit, it is true that pork is leaner and more versatile than ever before. The leanest cuts include the tenderloin, center and top loin chops, boneless sirloin chops and the boneless loin roast. Many "new" pork preparations, like the one on this page, are easy, fast and, if you've trimmed the fat, healthy. Not to mention delicious.

SKEWER TIP

If you're making kebobs and are using bamboo (not metal) skewers, soak them first in water for 20 minutes before threading on the chunks of food. This will prevent the wood from scorching.

pineapple are skewered and grilled with a maple/butter/orange glaze. The mushrooms are especially delicious, for they really soak up the flavor of the glaze.

8 small new potatoes (or 1 large baking potato cut into 8 chunks)
2 carrots, cut into 8 chunks (about 2 inches each)
1 - 1 ½ pounds lean pork (tenderloin, loin chops, etc.)
8 whole large mushrooms
1 small green or red bell pepper, cut into four pieces
8 chunks fresh pineapple

Maple Glaze:

4 tablespoons pure maple syrup
4 tablespoons butter
1 ½ teaspoons grated orange peel

Hot white rice (optional)

1. Prepare coals for outdoor grilling.
2. Parboil potatoes and carrots until barely tender. Cut the pork into 12 equal-size chunks.
3. Prepare the glaze by heating maple syrup, butter and orange peel until butter is melted.
4. Carefully spear the vegetables and pork onto long skewers.
5. Grill over hot coals, turning frequently and basting with the glaze, until done. This will take 10-16 minutes, depending upon the thickness of the pork.
6. If desired, serve on a bed of hot white rice.

Richard J. King
Mother King's Maple Syrup
Spring Green, Wisconsin

Wisconsin Choucroute
6 servings

"Choucroute" (pronounced shoo-kroot) is French for sauerkraut. This Wisconsin version of an earthy Alsatian favorite based on sauerkraut is very easy and wickedly good. After a chilly spree at the autumn market, get this combination of pork chops, sausage, sauerkraut and dark beer going in your crockpot, and enjoy it hours later when the sun goes down.

Its creator has even been known to satisfy her craving for its hearty flavors in summer: "I close all the windows and turn on the air conditioner full blast. It's really a BIG meal," says Mary Dolan. Accompanied by boiled potatoes, a simple green salad and some of the same good beer that's in the stew, Mary's Wisconsin Choucroute is wonderful, solid fare.

I like the heft of a bock beer in this dish, but Mary also suggests trying white wine. She recommends a dry Riesling or a spicy Gewurztraminer. (By the way, this meal tastes even more fabulous on the second day.)

Sauerkraut: 1 packed quart, homemade (see page 62); OR two bags (each 2 pounds), store-bought
1 tablespoon olive oil
1 tablespoon butter
1 large onion, sliced
1 bottle (12 ounces) bock or dark beer OR 1½ cups white wine
1 teaspoon fennel seeds
3 bay leaves
Cracked black pepper
1 pound kielbasa (Polish sausage), smoked bratwurst or veal sausage—cut into 2-inch pieces
4 loin pork chops (1½ - 2 pounds)
¼ pound bacon or ham, cut into 2-inch pieces
1 tart apple, peeled and chopped (optional)

Boiled potatoes, hot

1. Rinse sauerkraut well in a colander; drain and press out excess liquid.
2. Melt olive oil and butter in a heavy pot. Add onion and cook slowly until wilted. Stir in sauerkraut, beer or wine, fennel, bay leaves and plenty of cracked black pepper.

TRIM THE FAT

There are several things you can do to reduce the fat when preparing choucroute (recipe this page): Parboil the sausage for several minutes, then prick with a fork and drain well. Make sure the chops are well trimmed, and fry the bacon until crispy before draining it on paper towels and adding it to the pot. Before serving, you can also drain off the liquid from the pot into a bowl. Let it stand until the fat rises to the surface, then skim it off. Return the liquid to the pot and reheat.

FULL OF ENERGY
Bio-Cosmic
Agriculture

From Gene Litmiller, consultant for Farm-In-Balance, an organization that studies and promotes Bio-Cosmic Agriculture:

"We use the free energy that nature has put all around us to benefit the crops and livestock living in a certain area. The land is radiated with the cosmic energies all of the time. . . With heavy, polluted clouds in our sky, the cosmic energy is less.

We use energy wheels— like the ones American Indians built and used until the white man destroyed them; also cosmic pipes, etc. They are instruments that will measure energy and broadcast this energy to specific animals, land, etc.

There is much difference in the energy levels of various foods. Food harvested straight from the natural garden will be much higher [in energy] than that harvested from a garden that has had salt, fertilizers, chemicals, pesticides, etc. used on it. What is the difference? We must eat food that has a higher energy level than our bodies have or it will take energy from our bodies to digest the food."

3. Layer meats and sauerkraut mixture in a crockpot, starting and finishing with sauerkraut. Cover and cook on low 5-8 hours. The apple may be added during the last hour or two of cooking. The meat will be very tender (the pork should be falling off the bones—break it into chunks). Add additional black pepper to taste.
4. To serve: Place boiled potatoes in soup plates (low, flat bowls). Mash and ladle on the stew.

Mary Dolan
Formerly of Madison, Wisconsin

Lamb Riblets or Chops with Garlic and Wine
2 servings

Each summer I pack my freezer with lamb cuts from the Carpenters—Mary and Quentin—who offer their specialties at the Dane County Farmers' Market. Here's a great way to prepare the lamb riblets that come with each half-lamb order. This method would also work with other cuts of lamb like shoulder chops or shanks. Don't worry about the large amount of garlic—it mellows to a mild, unctuous paste that thickens and flavors the sauce.

The recipe may be doubled.

1 ½ **pounds lamb riblets or shoulder chops**
1 **tablespoon olive oil**
10-12 **garlic cloves, unpeeled**
¼-½ **cup chicken stock**
½ **cup dry white wine**
Salt and freshly ground black pepper

1. Trim lamb of as much fat as possible. Cut into serving-size pieces. In heavy pan with tight-fitting lid, heat oil and brown lamb on both sides.
2. Reduce heat to very low, add unpeeled garlic cloves and enough stock to cover the bottom of the pan. Cover pan. Simmer 45 minutes or longer, depending on the cut of the meat, until lamb is very tender. Add a little more stock if needed as it cooks.
3. Remove lamb and reserve. Pour garlic cloves and hot liquid into a separate bowl. Pour wine into the pot, raise heat and simmer hard, scraping up any bits on bottom of pan, until liquid begins to get syrupy. Turn off heat, let liquid rest a few minutes, then skim off any visible fat.
4. Skim off any fat that has risen to the surface of the garlic liquid. Pass the softened garlic and its liquid through a strainer back into the pot, pressing through as much of the garlic "meat" as possible. (Alternately, you may remove the skins and mash the garlic to a paste before adding it and any liquid back to the pan.) Sauce will be thin, but can be thickened by reducing further. Season to taste with salt and pepper.
5. Return lamb to pot and heat through. Serve with red potatoes, rice or Middle Eastern Stuffed Tomatoes (page 36).

MARY HAD A LITTLE LAMB

People who say they don't like lamb are probably really talking about mutton. What they describe as "strong-flavored" or "gamey" is nothing at all like the juicy, savory meat that's available from some local farmers. Tender lamb chops, cooked to medium rare, or braised shanks, simmered to the falling-off-the-bones stage, can outdo bland beef or chicken any day.

If you're looking for locally- and humanely-raised lamb or other meats, check out your nearest farmers' market. (Even if no one there carries it, they're likely to know someone who does.) Farmers like Mary and Quentin Carpenter of Fort Atkinson, Wisconsin offer lamb cuts, along with a variety of garden produce, at Madison's Saturday market. Each spring, a limited number of lucky people can also order their grain-fed lamb, a half-or whole one, cut to specification.

FAIR FOWL

A growing number of outdoor markets are making locally-raised, free-range chickens available to their customers. At several farmers' markets throughout Wisconsin you can also find duck, quail, turkey and pheasant. Because of the chemicals and inhumane treatment at many commercial operations, it's a good idea to purchase organically-raised meats and fowl. Fresh fowl purchased at the farmers' market is more expensive than the "factory" fowl from the grocery store. It is also healthier, meatier and tastier. Perhaps the higher price can serve to encourage us to limit our meat consumption—and that's a good idea, too—for our health and the health of the earth.

Duck with Tart Cherry Orange Glaze
4 servings

This recipe uses a straightforward, do-ahead method that ensures moist and tender duck without excess fat. Glazed with a brandy-accented reduction of tart cherries and orange marmalade, Duck with Tart Cherry Orange Glaze is very special, yet easy to execute.

Steps 1 and 2 can be done ahead of time. The final cooking time takes less than a half hour. If tart cherries are not available, substitute ¾ cup cherry preserves.

2 ducklings, each 2-3 pounds, fully thawed, giblets, neck and any fat pockets removed
Salt
1 orange, halved
1 onion, halved
Cracked black pepper

Sauce:

1 cup pitted tart cherries (fresh, or frozen and thawed) OR ¾ cup cherry preserves
½ cup orange marmalade
1 tablespoon bottled salsa or picante sauce
2 tablespoons brandy
⅛ teaspoon ground cloves

1. Preheat oven to 350 degrees. Salt ducks, inside and out. Place ½ orange and ½ onion inside each duck. Season ducks with pepper; place in a deep baking pan just large enough to hold them. Add enough water to cover bottom of pan. Cover tightly with foil. Bake 2-2½ hours, until tender (leg bone will twist easily in the meat). Remove ducks from pan and cool.
2. To make sauce: combine all ingredients in small saucepan. Simmer and stir until thickened, about 20 minutes. (If you are substituting cherry preserves for the whole cherries, simmering time will be shorter.) Puree in food processor or blender and cool.
3. To finish cooking: preheat oven to 400 degrees. Line a baking sheet with aluminum foil (can use the same foil you covered the ducks with). Split ducks in half lengthwise; cut out spine and remove rib cage; discard orange and onion halves. Place on baking sheet; bake 10 minutes. Brush on sauce; bake an additional 10-15 minutes. Serve immediately. The duck is delicious with wild rice (see page 135).

Irie Vibes Smoked Chicken
Yields one smoked chicken

When I splurge and buy an organically-raised chicken, I want a recipe that will do it justice. I found just the thing on the northern tip of Wisconsin, in Bayfield—not from a farm market vendor, but from a sailor. David Thom, owner of a 45-foot sailing yacht, offers chartered cruises in the waters of Lake Superior's romantic Apostle Islands. He serves his passengers a remarkably delicious chicken smoked with tea, cinnamon, orange and anise. His land-locked customers get a taste of this outstanding dish during Bayfield's annual Apple Festival, when David sets up a roadside stand to help feed the tourist throngs.

Developed from gourmet cookbooks, David's recipe calls for some unusual ingredients that may require a trip to a natural food store or oriental market. Or, you can order the packaged seasoning and smoking mixes (and a cruise) directly from David Thom of Irie Vibes, 410 Eichenwald Street, St. Paul, MN 55106.

An initial but very easy "dry-marinating" of the chicken is required 1-2 days in advance of cooking it. Serve Irie Vibes Smoked Chicken hot or, better yet, cooled to room temperature, when more of the smoky flavor comes through. For a special effect, present it whole—for picnics or cold buffets—flanked with orange wedges, red grapes and a sharp knife for serve-yourself slicing. Watch out, because it will quickly become the center of attention.

One 3-pound chicken, rinsed and patted dry, inside and out

Seasoning Mix:

2½ tablespoons coarse salt
1 tablespoon Szechuan peppercorns
1 teaspoon bottled dried orange peel
½ teaspoon onion powder
½ teaspoon ginger powder

Smoking Mix:

4-6 large cinnamon sticks
½ cup brown sugar
½ cup raw white rice
¼ cup black tea leaves
24 star anise points (break up 3 whole anise stars)
2 teaspoons bottled dried orange peel

■ ■ ■ ■ ■ ■ ■ ■ ■ ■

"Though I am by no means a vegetarian, I dislike the thought that some animal has been made miserable to feed me. If I am going to eat meat, I want it to be from an animal that has lived a pleasant, uncrowded life outdoors, on bountiful pasture, with good water nearby in order and trees for shade. . . A significant part of the pleasure of eating is in one's accurate consciousness of the lives and the world from which food comes."

Wendell Berry, in his essay, "The Pleasures of Eating"

Equipment:

Coffee grinder, blender, or mortar and pestle
Vegetable steamer
Kettle-type charcoal grill
Two small disposable foil pans—about 4 by 5 inches (can be made from sheets of aluminum foil)

1. To make seasoning mix: Heat coarse salt and Szechuan peppercorns in a heavy skillet over medium heat until salt begins to darken and you can smell the fragrant peppercorns. Cool slightly and grind to a powder in a coffee grinder, blender or mortar and pestle. Stir in 1 teaspoon dried orange peel, the onion powder and ginger powder.
2. To marinate chicken: Rub seasoning mix over outside and inside of chicken, cover and refrigerate at least 24 hours but not longer than 48 hours.
3. To cook chicken: Bring an inch of water to boil in a large pot fitted with a steamer. Position chicken on steamer, cover tightly and steam 30 minutes.
4. While chicken is steaming, prepare grill according to manufacturer's instructions for the indirect method of cooking. Prepare smoking mix by grinding cinnamon sticks to a coarse powder and combining this with remaining smoking mix ingredients. Divide smoking mix between the foil pans.
5. After chicken has steamed, place foil pans directly on hot coals. (DO NOT put smoking mix directly on coals without using the foil pans.) Place chicken on grill, cover, and partially close vents to reduce heat to medium (325-350 degrees). Smoke chicken 30 minutes. Close all vents; leave lid on 5 minutes longer. Chicken will be very dark. May be served immediately, but is also excellent at room temperature.

Captain David Thom
Irie Vibes Charters
St. Paul, Minnesota and Bayfield, Wisconsin

■ ■ ■ ■ ■ ■ ■ ■ ■ ■

Summer Sausage and Fried Onion on Rye
2 servings

Shoppers at many of the state's markets find more than fresh produce to tempt them. Occasionally, the special sausages of local butchers are available—meats like smoked kielbasa, bratwurst, liver sausage and summer sausage. Here's a summer sausage sandwich that really says "Wisconsin." Wash it down with a frosty cold beer or a tall glass of milk.

1-2 teaspoons butter or margarine
2 cups sliced yellow onions
Salt and freshly ground black pepper
3 ounces thin-sliced summer sausage (with or without garlic)
4 slices good rye bread or 2 rye rolls
Coarse-grained or brown mustard
1 tomato, sliced thick
Sliced dill pickles

1. Heat butter or margarine in large skillet. Add onions and cook over medium heat until wilted and golden brown. Season with salt and pepper. Push onions to one side of the pan, and "grill" sausage slices on both sides briefly.
2. Spread rye bread or rolls with mustard. Layer on the sausage, onions, tomato slices and pickles. Press well so it all holds together, and dig in.

THE MAD RUSH

For most, the farmers' market conjures up notions of leisurely shopping amid bounty and goodwill. But sometimes it's a rat race out there, especially when the rush is on for a hot item. Amy Van Ooyen, a market vendor in Hurley, Wisconsin, explains:

"Our manager sets the rules for the market. The hardest one is NO SELLING before 10 a.m. Folks come early and beg. The last ten minutes is torture for the customer and the sellers. Eyes are on that nice cabbage or cauliflower. Some lay a fat squash, a nice bunch of parsley, a couple cukes in front of them on the ground. They stand at attention, toes pointed, guarding their treasures until the signal. It's a mad rush, but who cares? It's fun. In about 30 minutes, our selection is gone."

ALL ABOUT BISON

One of the most surprising products cropping up at Wisconsin markets these days is buffalo meat. High in protein and nutrients, and low in fat and cholesterol— lower in fact, than turkey or chicken—buffalo meat is lean, tender and richly flavored. It resembles beef more than anything else, without any of the strong taste of some wild game.

The American buffalo is not a true buffalo (as water buffalo are), but is actually a member of the Bovidae family of mammals. It's more accurately called bison. They once roamed the plains in numbers so great it was practically unimaginable, but faced extinction by the late 1800s. Today, through the efforts of conservationists and ranchers, bison are off the endangered species list and number over 80,000 in public and private herds.

Cherokee Bison of Colby, Wisconsin offers naturally-raised bison at the Dane County Farmers Market, and will also ship the cuts frozen. Since bison contains very little marbling (fat within the muscle), the meat cooks more rapidly than beef. It can substitute for beef in any recipe, but use a lower-than-usual temperature and a shorter cooking time, and take precaution not to overcook it or it will dry out.

Turkey Mushroom Meatloaf
6 servings

A number of the ingredients in this recipe might be found at the local market, but even with store-bought ingredients, this is a meatloaf you'll make again and again. The ground turkey makes it healthier than beef or pork versions. Sage and rosemary give a "Thanksgiving" flavor, bacon adds smokiness and fresh mushrooms lend moistness. You'll want to make enough for meatloaf sandwiches the next day.

2 teaspoons vegetable or canola oil
2 cups finely chopped mushrooms (about ⅓ pound)
2 pounds ground turkey
¾ cup oat bran
½ cup minced onion
1 egg, lightly beaten
1 teaspoon dried rosemary OR 1 tablespoon fresh rosemary
1 teaspoon dried sage OR 1 tablespoon fresh sage
1 teaspoon salt
½ teaspoon pepper
4 slices bacon

1. Heat oven to 350 degrees. Heat oil in skillet and cook mushrooms over high heat until all moisture has evaporated.
2. Combine with remaining ingredients (except bacon) and form into an oval-shaped loaf. Top with strips of bacon. Place in baking dish; bake 1 hour. Let stand 10 minutes before serving.

Door County Fish Boil
4 servings

Once at a late-season farmers' market, I came upon a 20-pound bag of undersized onions, priced at a mere $1. Maybe the vendor thought no one would go for this sack of smaller-than-golf-ball vegetables, but I felt as if I'd just found the proverbial pearl in the oyster. Inspired, I imagined all the special dishes I'd prepare with those petite globes: shimmering glazed onions; beef stew with baby onions and mushrooms; marinated vegetables, skewered and grilled; and, best of all, a real fish boil, Door County-style.

Here's an indoor, home-sized version of Door County Fish Boil that works with any firm-fleshed fish steaks. (Whitefish or lake trout are traditional, but salmon is also delicious.) You can't get these fish at the farmers' market, but look there for new potatoes and baby onions—they're the authentic additions to fish boil. If these smaller vegetables are unavailable, use quartered large ones.

6 tablespoons salt, divided
12-16 small red potatoes, uniform in size
8 onions, same size as potatoes (or substitute 2 large onions)
8 chunks (2 inches thick) whitefish, lake trout or salmon steaks (1-2 pounds total)
Melted butter
Lemon wedges

1. Bring 1 gallon water and 3 tablespoons salt to boil in large pot over highest heat.
2. Scrub potatoes; cut off a small piece of peel from two opposite ends of each potato. Add to pot and boil vigorously 12 minutes.
3. Meanwhile, peel onions, leaving root ends intact. (If using large onions, clip off the top end, peel and carefully quarter the onions through the root ends.) Add onions to potatoes; boil 5 minutes.
4. Add remaining salt and the chunks of fish. Boil 10 minutes, then drain well, and portion on plates. Open each potato with a spoon or fork. Drizzle melted butter over all and serve with lemon wedges. The official Door County accompaniments are cole slaw, rye bread and tart cherry pie.

WHAT'S IN A NAME

To the uninitiated, "fish boil" doesn't sound too delectable. But if you're familiar with this Door County tradition, the phrase will make you salivate. You'll remember the fresh flavors of whitefish, red potatoes and baby onions boiled over an outdoor wood fire, drizzled with butter and served with rye bread, cole slaw and homemade cherry pie. You'll recall the smoke-and-pine-scented air, the snap of a cold beer on a dry throat, and the changing light of a tired sun on the beach sands.

Fish boils are a uniquely Wisconsin specialty. One of the best places to experience one is in Door County, where the tradition originated on the fishing tugs of Lake Michigan. Once a common dish for Native Americans and Scandinavian settlers, boiled lake fish is part of the cultural heritage of Wisconsin. But it was the commercial fishermen of Door County who brought their cooking skills to local events, staging the first community fish boils. Eventually area restaurateurs began offering the popular meal to tourists, and today, you haven't really experienced Door County until you've tasted a fish boil.

RAINBOWS ON YOUR PLATE

Pan-sized rainbow trout, farm-raised in Wisconsin, is available at some grocery stores and at a very reasonable price compared to most other seafood. If you want it super-fresh and direct from the source, buy it at the farmers' markets in Green Bay or Madison. Or what about your own town's farm market? Encourage the market manager to find a source for fresh trout.

The best way to treat fresh trout is to treat it simply. Stuff small-sized rainbows (8-10 ounces) with sprigs of fresh herbs, a sprinkling of salt and pepper and perhaps some thin slices of lemon. Oil the fish and your outdoor grill (or use an oiled grill basket, if available). Cook 4-6 minutes over hot coals in a covered grill, turn carefully and continue to cook until just tender, about another 4-6 minutes. If fish is thicker than 1 inch, it will take longer. Check for doneness by inserting a knife in the fish and lifting the flesh a little. It should look opaque, not transluscent, and moist, not dry.

Extra, Extra Trout with Avocado Yogurt Sauce
4 servings

Grilled, poached, steamed or baked, rainbow trout is a delicately-flavored fish that must not be overcooked nor masked with heavy sauces. Here's an unusual and very healthful method found in a British cookbook. The trout is wrapped in newspaper and steam-baked, then served with a simple avocado yogurt sauce. Note how neatly the fish skin comes off the flesh when you peel away the newspaper.

1 medium avocado, very ripe
2 teaspoons fresh lemon juice
¾ cup plain, no-fat yogurt
Freshly ground black pepper
4 rainbow trout (each 8 ounces), cleaned and gutted
1 small lemon, thinly sliced
1 small bunch fresh herbs: dill, parsley, cilantro, etc.
4 full sheets newspaper

1. To prepare sauce: Mash avocado and mix until smooth with lemon juice, yogurt and pepper to taste. Chill thoroughly.
2. To cook trout: Preheat oven to 350 degrees. Stuff each fish with lemon slices and sprigs of fresh herbs. Tightly wrap trout in individual sheets of newspaper, then thoroughly soak each package in cold water. Bake directly on oven rack until paper is dried out, 20-30 minutes.
3. To serve: With a scissors, cut each package open and peel off the paper (the fish skin will come off also). Carefully transfer the fish fillets (they will easily come away from the bones) to plates and serve immediately with the sauce.

Romeo's Rainbow Mousse
Makes 2-3 cups

Lightly smoked, farm-raised rainbow trout is hard to pass up, especially when it's fresh from the source. It's a little expensive, but here's a way to stretch the extravagance.

12-16 ounces smoked rainbow trout
1 medium onion
1 package (8 ounces) cream cheese or Neufchatel, softened
Bottled hot pepper sauce
Crackers

Carefully and thoroughly bone the smoked trout. Place in food processor. Chop onion; add to trout. Add the cream cheese; process until smooth and creamy. Season to taste with hot pepper sauce. Serve on crackers.

Matthew Terrance Romeo
Allen Creek Trout Farm
Oxford, Wisconsin

Smoked Fish Sandwich

The fish markets of Bayfield, Algoma, Gills Rock, Port Washington and more are suppliers of one of the greatest treats Wisconsin has to offer. Personally hooked on smoked fish of any kind, I think smoked Wisconsin lake trout and whitefish are as exotic and delicious as any delicacy from the ocean deep. Here's a very easy, very casual way to indulge.

Boned, flaked smoked whitefish or lake trout
Softened unsalted butter or low-fat cream cheese
Rye, pumpernickel or whole grain bread
Red onion, sliced very thin
Vine-ripened tomatoes, sliced thick
Leaf lettuce or alfalfa sprouts
Freshly ground black pepper (if desired)

For each sandwich: spread two slices bread with butter or cream cheese. On one slice, pile on as much smoked fish as you care or dare. Layer with thin red onion circles, juicy tomato slices and some lettuce or alfalfa sprouts. Lots of freshly ground black pepper is wonderful, too. Top with the other slice of bread, press gently and dig in.

"When you shop without awareness, you fall prey to the tyranny of the everyday, caught in the deadening perception of mechanical routine and boredom. But when you shop consciously, you experience a sense of wonder and delight at the abundance of available foods. You also practice discrimination by selecting the healthiest foods, rather than those that are simply attractively packaged. Experiencing sensory aliveness and exercising discernment help convert a seemingly routine experience into a subtle, nonrepeatable exercise in wakefulness."

Spiritual writer
David Spangler

Smoked Trout with Horseradish Cream

A very decadent version of the smoked fish sandwich in the previous recipe; this one should be served as an appetizer. Again no measurements are given, for it is up to you how thick to spread the butter, how high to stack the fish and how sharply to season the horseradish cream.

Cocktail-size rye bread
Butter (unsalted preferred)
Red onion, sliced very thin
Smoked lake or rainbow trout, boned
1 or 2 lemon wedges
Heavy (or whipping) cream, unsweetened and unfla-
**   vored, whipped to stiff peaks (see side bar, page 70)**
Freshly grated or prepared horseradish

For garnish: parsley sprigs and more lemon wedges

Butter bread slices. Line with thinly sliced red onion. Top with chunks of smoked fish. Squeeze a few drops of lemon juice over fish. Fold horseradish into unsweetened whipped cream, to reach desired hotness. Place a dollop of horseradish cream on each sandwich. These are beautiful on a silver platter garnished with lemon wedges and parsley sprigs. Serve at room temperature or chilled.

Smoked Whitefish and Potato Cakes
Makes eight to ten 3-inch cakes

Though one can find excellent, delicately-smoked rainbow trout at some farmers' markets, there's nothing like the messy opulence of Lake Michigan or Lake Superior smoked fish, at its freshest directly from a waterside market.

Whitefish or lake trout, it's delicious on its own, but if you want something a little different, try these patties of smoked fish, whipped potatoes, onions and horseradish. They're good at breakfast, brunch, lunch or dinner.

(continued on next page)

Smoked Whitefish and Potato Cakes *(continued)*

2 cups boned, flaked smoked whitefish or lake trout
   (about 1 pound before boning)
1½ cups mashed potatoes, cooled
3 tablespoons minced onion
2 tablespoons prepared horseradish (or to taste)
1 egg white
¼ teapoon white pepper
2 tablespoons butter or butter/oil combination
Sour cream, sour half-and-half or plain no-fat yogurt
Chopped fresh parsley

1. Mash smoked fish with fork and remove any stray
   bones. Combine with potatoes, onion, horseradish,
   egg white and pepper. Form into 3-inch patties (8-10
   total). Chill one hour.
2. Melt butter (or butter and oil) in large skillet. When hot,
   add patties and cook over medium heat 2-3 minutes.
   Carefully turn and cook on other side 3-4 minutes, until
   lightly browned. Serve with small dollops of sour
   cream or yogurt and a sprinkling of chopped parsley.
   Handle gently.

Whitefish Livers with Bacon, Onion and Mushrooms
2 main-course servings, 4-6 as appetizer

4 slices bacon, cut into 1-inch pieces
½ cup finely chopped onion
1 cup thin-sliced mushrooms
2 cups fresh whitefish livers, rinsed and drained
1 tablespoon butter
Salt and freshly ground black pepper
Chopped fresh parsley

1. Fry bacon pieces in a large skillet until crispy. Remove
   with slotted spoon and drain on paper towels. Discard
   all but 2 tablespoons of the fat.
2. Add onion to pan and cook over low heat 3 minutes.
   Raise heat to high, add mushrooms and cook until
   tender. Set mushroom mixture aside in a bowl.
3. Heat butter in same skillet, add livers and cook over
   medium heat until just tender and still slightly pink in
   the middle, 4-7 minutes. Stir in the mushroom mixture
   during last minute of cooking.
4. Season to taste with salt and pepper. Garnish with
   chopped fresh parsley. Serve immediately.

WHITEFISH LIVERS

You won't find whitefish
livers at any inland farmers'
market, but if you ever get
up to the picturesque town
of Bayfield on Lake
Superior, cross your fingers
and hope that one of the
local fish markets will have
some fresh ones available
that day. Milder in flavor
than beef or chicken liver,
whitefish livers are a real
delicacy in that fishing-and-
tourist town. Served at local
restaurants like Gruenke's,
which lays claim to the
popularization of these
unusual morsels, whitefish
livers are prepared in the
same way as other livers—
lightly breaded and sautéed,
pureed in a pâté, or
combined with bacon,
onion and mushrooms, as
in the recipe on this page.

GIVING GOOD WEIGHT
The Green Bay Farmers' Market

News of the big war filled local papers back in 1917. Nevertheless, the opening of a public market in town made the front page that year in the Green Bay Press Gazette. The headlines read: "Success Attends Formal Opening of City Market; Business is Quite Brisk."

The market that started at a small park on Green Bay's near east side is still alive and very healthy in the 1990s. Over 300 people attended the first market on September 1, 1917; now, a typical Saturday sees 5000-plus customers, with another several thousand coming to the Wednesday market across the Fox River on the west side of town.

The first market, initiated during a war economy, had one simple purpose: "To reduce food costs." Not a word during those days about environmentalism or saving the farms. Product variety was limited to vegetables like corn, tomatoes, cabbage and apples. Today, those basic items are still the most popular purchases, but there's also room for more exotic things like dried herbs, fresh flowers, shiitake mushrooms and farm-raised trout.

One thing that's been consistent through the years of the Green Bay market is its management. Most farmers' markets are government-regulated, but are operated by business organizations or non-profit groups. In Green Bay, however, market management has been handled directly by a city official from the start. In 1917, Mayor Elmer S. Hall appointed City Sealer of Weights and Measures John Kelleher to act as general manager of the new market. Providing one of the oldest governmental services, the City Sealer was responsible for maintaining accurate weights and measures in all city commerce. The task of operating the market was a natural extension of that position, and after more than three-quarters of a century, that's where the responsibility still lies.

Today, Green Bay's City Sealer, the man who makes sure vendors "give good weight," is Dan Kryzanek. "Inspecting weights isn't a very big part of the market job anymore," says Dan. "I spend more time at the market just helping things run smoothly." His predecessor in 1917 posted signs in neighboring towns to encourage farmers to come sell their produce, but Dan has the opposite problem: "People would give their right arm for a stall; I mostly have to fight them off. Some vendors have been here 25, 35 years." He laughs and adds: "Stall permits are more valuable than Packer tickets during the glory years."

What does he do to bring customers in? "Very little," is Dan's comment. "It's just not necessary; they come in droves! We couldn't keep them away if we tried. It's actually amazing how much the market has grown, all on its own, in the past years."

Wisconsin weather forces most markets to open as late as mid-summer, for that's when there's enough ripe vegetables to make the farmers' trip to town worthwhile. In Green Bay, the market begins around the second week of July and lasts into November. If the weather also lasts, that is.

Rules about what can be sold at markets vary throughout the state; in Green Bay you can't

find any prepared or processed foods, but you can get homemade crafts. Of course, there's exceptions to the rules. Honey is an acceptable processed food; so are dried herbs.

Dan also closely regulates the crafts, keeping the main emphasis on fresh produce. "That's really what the market is all about," says Dan. "Food. Good, fresh food at a good price."

Now that sounds like something they would have said in 1917.

Fresh Market
W·I·S·C·O·N·S·I·N

DAIRY AND EGGS

Layered Chèvre and Coriander Pesto
Makes 2 cups

Fresh plain chèvre is a delicious substitute for cream cheese, and it makes a velvety complement to ingredients more assertive in flavor and texture. An imaginative example of this comes from Jessica Carneol of Renaissance Farms, where she and co-owner Mark Olson grow acres of fragrant basil and coriander. Jessica layers deep green coriander pesto with a blend of chèvre and cream cheese, tinted pale pink by a little salsa. It makes a beautiful and intensely flavorful appetizer.

Served at the 1991 Fall Harvest Tasting in Madison (sponsored by the Dane County Farmers' Market), Jessica's creation drew a reaction from the festival's guest of honor, Julia Child. Julia's comment? "M-m-m-m-m-m!!"

6 ounces goat cheese (plain), at room temperature
1 package (8 ounces) cream cheese, softened
3 tablespoons bottled salsa
1 cup coriander pesto (recipe on page 129)

Cilantro sprigs (fresh coriander) for garnish
Plain crackers

1. Beat goat cheese and cream cheese until smooth. Fold in salsa.
2. Line a shallow, round 3-cup mold or dish with large, overlapping sheets of plastic wrap, enough to hang several inches over the edges of the dish. Spread alternating layers of cheese mixture and pesto in the dish, beginning and ending with the cheese (four layers of cheese, three of pesto). Don't worry about getting perfect edges, for you can smooth them later when the cheese is unmolded. Fold plastic wrap over the top. Chill 4-8 hours or overnight.
3. To serve, unfold the wrap, place a serving plate face down over the mold and turn upside to unmold the spread. Peel off the plastic wrap. Smooth the edges of the spread with a knife. Garnish, if desired, with fresh coriander leaves. Serve with plain crackers.

Jessica Carneol and Mark Olson
Renaissance Farms
Spring Green, Wisconsin

SAY CHÈVRE

Fantome Farm of Ridgeway is one of the few producers of chèvre—or goat cheese—in the United States. Lower in fat than many cheeses, Fantome Farm's chèvre (pronounced shevr) has an earthy tang and comes in a variety of forms: soft and spreadable, combined with garlic, chives or cracked black pepper; or denser and super-creamy, steeped in olive oil. Sometimes tiny logs are rolled in edible ash. Look for Fantome Farm's stand at the Dane County Farmer's Market in Madison, and stock up—the soft varieties freeze well and make a delicious spread for crackers, sandwiches, fresh vegetables, fish or chicken.

IT'S A STRING THING

String cheese is Wisconsin's answer to fun food. These crayon-sized cylinders of cheese are eaten by stripping or shredding them with your fingers and popping the mild, salty threads into your mouth. Fifteen years ago they were available only from out-of-the-way cheese factories, but today they're in the dairy case of every grocery store. If you're lucky enough to have a cheese vendor at your local farmers' market, you'll find string cheese there, too. Convenient for snacking, they can also be used in these creative ways:

- stripped to pile on sandwiches;
- sliced into thin rounds to add to salads;
- rolled into slices of ham that have been spread lightly with cream cheese, then cut into rounds for appetizers;
- cut into chunks and skewered with cherry tomatoes or melon wedges;
- stripped to add to pasta salad, seafood salad or hearty soups.

Bobby Rodriguez's Marinated String Cheese
Makes 1½ cups

I never thought about using string cheese in a recipe until I met Bobby Rodriguez, a Door County musician and gourmet cookshop operator. Bobby says he gets his culinary inspirations after late-night gigs when he's hungry and too keyed up to sleep. Sometimes he makes a simple salad of string cheese, lemon juice and herbs, and eats it as a side dish with tacos. I think it would be good in tacos, too, or on crackers or buttered bread, or in a tossed salad, or with most any meal.

6 ounces string cheese
Juice of 1 small lemon
Pinch of salt
1 teaspoon oregano or other dried herb
Freshly ground black pepper to taste
Celery or bell peppers (optional)

String the cheese (not too thinly), then cut into 2-inch lengths. Combine with lemon juice, salt, oregano and pepper. If desired, you can also add some "stringed" celery, or minced bell peppers. Marinate in refrigerator, tossing occasionally, until ready to serve. The flavor improves with age.

Bobby Rodriguez
The Cookbook
Ephraim, Wisconsin

Cheddar Cheese Soufflé
2-4 servings

You may not think of soufflé as a Wisconsin tradition, but this recipe from Esther Schrock of Glen Flora has been in her family, she says, "ever since I can remember, and I'm 72 years old!" Esther bakes a soufflé when she has leftover cheese that's gotten a little hard or dry. While any type will do, I think a well-aged Cheddar gives the best Dairyland flavor.

(continued on next page)

Cheddar Cheese Soufflé *(continued)*

If you've not baked soufflés before, don't be wary, but do read through all the instructions before you begin. The cheese sauce that is used as the base of the soufflé is practically foolproof, and it can wait for you until you're ready to whip the egg whites. Allow no interruptions while you are doing Step 2, and pop the soufflé into a hot oven immediately after folding in the beaten egg whites.

If you'd like, chopped fresh herbs or a light tomato sauce may accent each serving of soufflé.

3 tablespoons butter
3 tablespoons flour
1 cup milk
1 bay leaf
1 cup finely grated extra sharp Cheddar cheese
½ teaspoon salt
⅛ teaspoon ground white pepper
Pinch of nutmeg
3 eggs

1. To make soufflé base: Melt butter in small pan over low heat; stir in flour and cook 3-4 minutes, stirring often. Heat milk (do not boil) and whisk it into the pan. Raise heat to medium and stir until sauce is thick and smooth. Add bay leaf and simmer over very low heat 10 minutes. Remove from heat and stir in cheese, a little at a time, until sauce is smooth again; season with salt, white pepper and nutmeg. Cool at least 10 minutes. Remove bay leaf. Separate eggs; stir egg yolks into cooled base. Let egg whites come to room temperature (they will whip better this way).
2. To finish and bake: Preheat oven to 350 degrees; generously grease a round, 4-cup baking dish. Whip egg whites until stiff peaks form. Lighten the cheese base by stirring in ¼ of the beaten egg whites with a spatula. Gently fold in the remaining egg whites, again with a spatula. Don't overdo it; a few streaks or small bumps remaining in the mixture is fine. Gently turn mixture into baking dish and place in oven.
3. Bake 35-40 minutes, until firm and high. Bring to table, allow one or two "oohs" and "ahs," then serve immediately.

Esther Schrock
Glen Flora, Wisconsin

TRICK OR TREAT

The only real trick to soufflés is getting your dinner companions seated before the soufflé comes out of the oven, so they are present for its brief but impressive moment of puffed wonder.

ENVIRONMENT-FRIENDLY MARKETING

Looking for ways to get "environmental?" The place to go is the farmers' market. That's where you can find pesticide-free foods, save on fuel and resources and avoid wasteful packaging. Here's some more ideas for earth-conscious marketing:

Reuse: plastic bags, paperbags

Return: egg cartons, berry boxes, maple syrup jugs, potting containers

Recycle: glass bottles, jars, plastic cider jugs

Compost: corn husks, melon rinds, any vegetable scraps

Buy: only what you can consume, what's in season, organic produce, fresh flowers to dry

Cook: simply, in quantity— and freeze, can, dry, store

Travel: by bus, by bike, on foot

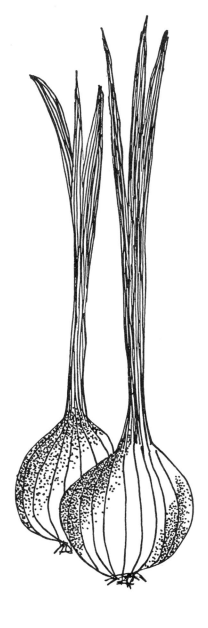

Swiss Onion Potato Bread
Makes one loaf

Swiss cheese, potatoes and sautéed onions have a wonderful affinity for one another in this easy, quick-to-make bread. The attractive round loaf bakes up golden brown; its aroma alone is worth your time. It's also a great way to use up leftover mashed potatoes.

1 tablespoon butter or olive oil
1 cup minced onion
1 teaspoon minced garlic
2 cups flour
1 tablespoon baking powder
½ teaspoon salt
1 cup mashed potatoes, chilled
4 ounces grated Swiss cheese (about 1½ cups)
¼ cup olive oil
1 egg
Milk

1. Heat 1 tablespoon butter or olive oil in small skillet; add onions and garlic. Cook slowly, stirring often, until onions are translucent. Cool thoroughly.
2. Heat oven to 375 degrees. Grease a 9-inch pie pan. Combine flour, baking powder and salt. Lightly work in mashed potatoes with your fingertips until mixture resembles fine meal. Lightly stir in grated Swiss cheese and cooled onions.
3. Measure ¼ cup olive oil in a measuring cup. Mix in egg. Add enough milk to make ⅔ cup, and stir until well combined. Make a well in center of flour mixture. Pour in liquid mixture and stir until dough just comes together, adding more milk only if necessary. Do not beat.
4. Turn dough onto a well-floured work surface and knead gently 10-12 times. Form into a smooth ball; place in pan and flatten gently to cover bottom of pan. Score lightly with a sharp knife in a pinwheel pattern, for 8 servings.
5. Bake 35-45 minutes, until golden brown and fully cooked in the center (toothpick inserted in center should come out clean). Serve warm or at room temperature.

■▓■▓■▓■▓■▓■▓■▓■▓■▓■▓■▓■▓
▓■▓■▓■▓■▓■▓■▓■▓■▓■▓■▓■▓■

Dolores's Cauliflower Cheese Casserole
6-8 servings

In this recipe, Dolores Sikora, manager of the deli at the sumptuous Elegant Farmer market in Mukwonago (see side bar, page 44), adds mushrooms and bacon bits to her mother's cauliflower/cheese casserole. I cut back on some of the butter, cheese and bacon, and still found this a rich and satisfying dish.

6 slices bacon, chopped
½ pound mushrooms, sliced
1-2 heads cauliflower (1 ½ pounds total)
2 tablespoons butter
⅔ cup chopped onion
Salt and freshly ground black pepper
1 heaping teaspoon flour
½ - 1 cup milk
6 ounces (about 2 cups) shredded Cheddar cheese
1 ½ tablespoons breadcrumbs

1. Fry bacon until crispy in a medium skillet. Drain on paper towels. Pour off all but 1 ½ tablespoons of the bacon fat from the pan. Add mushrooms and toss over medium-high heat until tender. Place mushrooms in a bowl and set aside (skillet will be used again).
2. Bring a large pot of salted water to boil. Cut cauliflower into flowerets. Add to boiling water and cook 4-5 minutes, until just tender. Drain and set aside. Preheat oven to 350 degrees.
3. In skillet used previously, melt butter, add onions and cook over medium heat until brown and tender. Season well with salt and pepper. Reduce heat, sprinkle in flour and stir over low heat 3-4 minutes. Whisk in enough milk to make a sauce and continue whisking until it thickens. Sprinkle in the cheese, stirring to smooth the sauce as the cheese melts. Add more milk if sauce becomes too thick. Taste, and adjust seasonings.
4. Layer cauliflower, mushrooms and bacon bits in a casserole. Pour cheese sauce over top and sprinkle with breadcrumbs. Bake 25-30 minutes. Serve immediately.

Dolores Sikora
The Elegant Farmer
Mukwonago, Wisconsin

"I tried out on him once an idea I had picked up in a vocational agriculture class. 'Farming,' I said to him, 'is after all, a business like any other. The purpose of farming is to make a living.'

He flew into a rage. 'Listen here, young man,' he said. 'The purpose of farming is to produce food for hungry people. It is a calling, not a living, and don't you ever forget it!'"

Paul Gruchow,
writing about his father
in the essay,
"Remember the Flowers"

COWS ON THE CONCOURSE

Every Wisconsinite worth his/her salt knows that June is Dairy Month, and the ones who live in or visit Madison make it a point to attend "Cows on the Concourse," a rather unusual dairy celebration that takes place on a Saturday each June.

On that day, vendors at the Dane County Farmers' Market make room on the Capitol Square for special guests with names like Bessie, Elsie and Bossie. Open-air tents set up near the produce stands house the visiting cows so market-goers can get an up-close bovine experience. Some city-types even try their hand at milking a cow for the first time.

Dairy treats of all kinds are offered by food vendors during the festival. Needless to say, the stands with the longest lines are the ones that serve cream puffs (see recipe this page).

Cream Puffs
Makes 16-20 three-inch puffs

Cream puffs get soggy easily, so serve them as soon as you can after they've cooled completely. To re-crisp leftovers, heat in a 375-degree oven for several minutes.

6 tablespoons butter
2 teaspoons sugar
⅛ teaspoon salt
1 cup flour
4 large eggs, at room temperature
Sweetened whipped cream (see side bar, page 70)
Powdered sugar

1. Preheat oven to 400 degrees. Grease two baking sheets. Combine 1 cup water, butter, sugar and salt in a heavy saucepan. Bring to a boil. Remove from heat and quickly stir in all the flour until a stiff ball forms. Return to medium heat and cook, stirring constantly, 2 minutes.
2. Remove again from the heat and let cool slightly. Break one egg into the dough and beat vigorously until smooth. Repeat this process until all the eggs are added. The dough will be smooth and glossy.
3. Spoon heaping tablespoonfuls of dough onto the baking sheets, spacing them well apart (or pipe the dough onto the sheets with a pastry bag).
4. Bake 5 minutes, then reduce heat to 375 degrees. Bake 20-25 minutes, until golden and puffed and firm to the touch. To dry out the egg-y insides of the puffs, vent each one by piercing it with a sharp knife along its side. Leave in oven, with the heat off and door ajar, until oven is cool. Remove and thoroughly cool puffs on a rack. To serve, cut in half horizontally, fill with real whipped cream and dust with powdered sugar.

Wisconsin Three Cheese Ball
Makes one large cheese ball

Paula Collins' Wisconsin Three Cheese Ball combines sharp Cheddar, crumbled blue cheese and cream cheese with another state specialty—horseradish, grown and bottled by Silver Springs Gardens in Paula's hometown of Eau Claire. "Wisconsin is not just famous for fine dairy products and contented cows," she writes, noting that Silver Springs is one of the largest producers of horseradish in the United States.

Paula's cheese ball recipe was first published in a New York Cooking and Crafts Club book titled "Holiday Home Cooking."

11 ounces cream cheese, softened to room temperature
4 ounces blue cheese, crumbled
1½ cups (about 5 ounces) shredded sharp Cheddar cheese
½ cup minced onion
2 tablespoons milk
2 tablespoons mayonnaise
1 tablespoon (or more) horseradish
1 tablespoon Worcestershire sauce
1 cup pecans, finely chopped

1. Place the cheeses in a mixing bowl. Add remaining ingredients, except pecans, and blend with electric beaters on low speed, scraping sides and bottom of bowl occasionally. Beat on medium speed until fluffy. Cover bowl and chill thoroughly (several hours to overnight).
2. Spread pecans on waxed paper. Shape the cheese mixture into a ball and roll it in the pecans. Chill two hours, until firm. Arrange on platter with crackers or fresh vegetables.

Paula Collins
Eau Claire, Wisconsin

SCENES FROM THE MARKET: Lake Mills

Heavy rains early in the morning keep most of the vendors away one September Saturday, though normally there's 50-60 farm stands lining the Lake Mills City Park at this time of the year. The sun is out by 9:30, however, and things get social:

• The open bed of a big green pickup holds a hill of carrots—fat, fresh and bright orange, with bushy green tops. "Hey, lookit this!" shouts a young boy as he selects a carrot—weirdly shaped like a pistol—from the load. He zaps invisible enemies in the vicinity. "Blam!"

• "Let me tell you about my recipe for sour cream cookies," remarks a small, elderly woman, nearly hidden behind her produce. "I make them every year at Christmas. Been making them every year, in fact, since 1939, the year I was married. I got the recipe from my sister-in-law." She pauses: "Both our husbands are gone now." Then a smile: "But we're still around and we're still making those cookies!"

• Another woman sells her homemade baked goods. "All original!" she emphasizes. When asked for recipes, she begins to chat:

"The kids ask me "Mom, how do you make this?' I tell them 'a little of this and a little of that.' They want to know exactly, want me to write it down. But I never do that. I just make it." Does she use any cookbooks? "I use a cookbook from back in 1907—The White Cookbook. They talk about a thimble of salt, an 'egg' of butter. I remember when cookbooks were like that. Course, don't get me wrong, I'm not THAT old. Not as old as 1907, anyway."

"Everything we own we owe to udders."

Sign on dairy barn
near Lake Mills, Wisconsin

Fresh Vegetable Gazpacho Eggs
6 servings

The Wisconsin Department of Agriculture sponsors annual recipe contests in conjunction with many state-based producers associations. Winning recipes get highlighted at food festivals and farmers' markets and in free recipe brochures. What a great way to promote the people and products of our state. A 1990 Junior Wisconsin Egg Cooking Contest yielded this first prize winner from student Travis Styer of Colfax.

Sauce:

¾ cup finely chopped tomato
¾ cup finely chopped zucchini (or try bell peppers)
¾ cup finely chopped cucumber
1 cup bottled salsa (mild, medium or hot—you decide)

Other Ingredients:

4 tablespoons margarine, butter or olive oil
1 cup finely chopped onions
12 eggs
Salt and black pepper to taste
1 cup shredded Cheddar cheese

1. To make sauce: Combine all sauce ingredients in small bowl. Set aside.
2. In large skillet (preferably non-stick), heat margarine, butter or oil. Add onions and sauté until tender.
3. Beat eggs with 2 tablespoons water in a large bowl. Pour into skillet; cook over medium heat 4-6 minutes. As edges set, tip pan and run a spatula around its edges to allow uncooked eggs to flow to bottom of skillet. Cover; cook an additional 2-3 minutes or until eggs are set.
4. Turn off heat, sprinkle eggs with cheese, and cover. Let stand a few minutes until cheese melts. To serve, cut into wedges and spoon sauce over each.

Travis Styer
Colfax, Wisconsin

GETTING THE CONNECTION
Community Supported Agriculture

There's a relatively new idea in direct marketing gaining ground these days, an idea that may go one better than the benefits available at farmers' markets. It's called Community Supported Agriculture (CSA) and it helps link growers and consumers in an innovative and meaningful way.

This is how CSA works: At the beginning of a season, farmers sell shares of their harvest to participants from in or around their community, who then collect their weekly "dividends" at designated pick-up points.

CSA provides the growers with a guaranteed market and some security against the financial risk that's threatening farms today. Buyers gain in many ways: Fresh, organic produce raised for its taste and nutritional content (as opposed to its ship-ability) is available in a convenient and cost-effective manner. Shareholders also participate in the decisions about what varieties are planted and how they're grown. In some cases, participants share the workload, too. Most importantly, they enjoy a direct connection to the food they eat and to the people who grow it.

Also known as subscription farming, community supported agriculture is typical in Japan and Europe. It's seeing great success on the East Coast and in California, and is now cropping up in Wisconsin, too.

Peter and Bernadette Seely run Springdale Farm, a successful subscription farm in Plymouth, about an hour north of Milwaukee. They offer farm-fresh organic vegetables and eggs to over 125 families ten months of the year. "We had to advertise in the beginning," says Bernadette. "Now there's a waiting list. Eighty percent of our participants are from Milwaukee, so we have seven pick-up points there, plus one in Sheboygan and one right at the farm. That's a little different from some CSAs, where the buyers are mostly from the immediate community."

At Springdale Farm, part-time workers help with the growing and harvesting of produce. "At first, it was just too much work," says Bernadette. "We eventually formed a core group of subscribers who help with organization and outreach tasks. That's been a real support for us, both emotionally and administratively."

The Seelys sponsor once-a-month events for subscribers at Springdale, "sometimes work-oriented, sometimes just for fun," notes Bernadette. "Barndances, garlic-braiding, things like that. It makes people feel good to be involved. They like getting the really fresh produce, but the community aspect of it makes them even more committed."

And commitment is what it's all about. The people who grow our food make up a mere 1% of our population, but their success or failure should be the concern of the 100% who depend on them for high quality, nutritious food. Community supported agriculture is a natural. It may even be a necessity.

If you live in southern Wisconsin and would like more information about CSAs—or if you'd like to join one—contact the Madison Area Community Supported Agriculture Coalition (MACSAC), c/o John Greenler, 2625 Oaklawn Rd., Stoughton, WI 53589, (608) 873-0637.

Fresh Market
W·I·S·C·O·N·S·I·N

HERBS, NUTS, WILD RICE AND POPCORN

Hot Herb Biscuits
Makes 6-8 biscuits

Nothing adds flavor like fresh herbs from the market. From the first lively snippets of dill in spring, to summer's basil-scented air, and on to the full harvest of flavors— sage, rosemary, thyme—in fall, fresh herbs add an unmatched dimension to foods through all the seasons.

Here's a recipe that can highlight any one of your favorite herbs. Try sage-flecked Hot Herb Biscuits with grilled pork chops or roast turkey. An accent of dill in your brunch biscuits goes nicely with smoked fish. Serving ham or creamed chicken? Add minced parsley to the biscuit dough.

For biscuit-baking guidelines, see side bar, page 73.

1¾ cups flour
3 teaspoons baking powder
½ teaspoon salt
4 tablespoons cold butter, cut into small pieces
2 tablespoons minced fresh herbs
¾ cup milk

1. Preheat oven to 450 degrees. Sift flour, baking powder and salt into a medium bowl. Cut in butter with a pastry cutter or two knives until pieces are the size of sunflower seeds.
2. Sprinkle herbs over the flour mixture, then make a well in the center. Pour in milk, stir gently a few strokes to distribute the milk, then stir quickly until dough pulls away from the sides of the bowl. This will only take a moment.
3. Turn dough onto a floured surface. Knead lightly and briefly (4-6 turns). Roll or pat to a thickness of 1 inch. Do not overwork the dough.
4. Cut with a 3-inch biscuit cutter into rounds or with a sharp knife into triangles. Gather dough scraps; reform and cut again, for a total of 6-8 biscuits.
5. Place in ungreased baking pan. Bake 13-14 minutes until high and golden brown. Serve warm. Freeze leftovers or store them airtight for they dry out quickly.

WHAT A BARGAIN

Price tags carry an almost hallowed authority with many of us; culturally-speaking, we're just not comfortable with dickering. But put your reluctance aside at farmers' markets, for you're likely to find a vendor willing to barter when:

- it's late in the day;
- it's peak season for the produce in mind;
- you're buying an item in bulk;
- you're a regular customer;
- you're buying a variety of items;
- the produce is undersized, oversized or blemished;
- there's only one or two left of the item.

PESTO MAGIC

Just a few years ago, pesto was a mysterious food to most of us, known only to gourmets and food magazine writers. But like quiche, pesto is now familiar and well-loved fare to many people. It's hard to beat for flavor and convenience.

Pesto is sold at some farmers' markets, but why not pick up a large bunch of herbs and make it yourself? While basil and pine nuts make the classic combination, other fresh herbs, nuts and cheeses can be substituted to create a variety of intensely-flavored sauces. Try young coriander leaves (cilantro), lemon basil or dill. Fresh parsley can be added to the mixture to lessen the intensity of the main herb. Replace the usual Parmesan with another hard cheese like Pecorino, Asiago or Romano. Pecans or walnuts can be substituted for expensive pine nuts.

Pesto freezes very well and can be used in many more ways than to sauce pasta. Try it on omelettes or steamed vegetables, in potato salad or spaghetti sauce, as a sandwich spread, on grilled fish and meats, in a creamy dip or dressing, or to top a soup.

Pesto
Makes about 1½ cups

Here's a framework recipe for many kinds of pesto. The addition of reduced chicken stock allows you to use less oil than what's in many pesto recipes. You may opt to skip the stock, however, and increase the amount of oil by several tablespoons.

1½ cups unsalted chicken stock (see side bar, page 54 for method)
2 cups tightly-packed fresh herbs (leaves only)
1 cup nutmeats
3-4 peeled garlic cloves
⅓ cup olive oil
½ - ¾ cup freshly grated Parmesan or other hard cheese
Freshly ground black pepper

Bring chicken stock to a hard simmer in a small saucepan. Reduce to ⅓ cup and cool to room temperature. Puree herbs, nuts and garlic in food processor or blender. With machine running, add olive oil in a thin stream. Turn off machine; add cooled stock, cheese and several grindings of pepper. Process briefly, until well combined. Refrigerate or freeze airtight to prevent discoloration. Serve at room temperature.

A Particularly Pleasant Pesto Pasta Salad
6-8 servings

Renaissance Farms of Spring Green has been selling organically-grown basil and fresh pestos for seven years at the Dane County Farmers' Market. Besides basil-based pesto, owners Mark Olson and Jessica Carneol market lemon basil and cilantro pestos throughout the upper Midwest. They use only the highest quality ingredients: virgin olive oil, 100% Parmesan and Romano cheeses, toasted pine nuts and fresh garlic. The taste says it all. You can add any of their line to this Particularly Pleasant Pasta Salad, or use your own excellent pesto.

(continued on next page)

½ cup pesto (recipe, page 129)
¼ cup freshly grated Parmesan or Romano cheese
3 tablespoons minced shallots, onion or green onion
3 tablespoons vinegar (your choice)
1-2 teaspoons minced garlic
½ teaspoon salt
¼ teaspoon ground black pepper
1 pound rotini (spiral) pasta, cooked and drained
1 medium red or green bell pepper, chopped
1 large ripe tomato, cut into chunks

Mix first 7 ingredients in a large bowl. Stir in pasta, bell peppers and tomato chunks. Chill and serve.

Jessica Carneol and Mark Olson
Renaissance Farms
Spring Green, Wisconsin

Herbed Potato Salad
8-10 servings

Old-fashioned potato salad, sparked with vinegar and creamy with mayonnaise, is updated by adding chopped fresh herbs. Carol Frank, who sent this recipe from the West Bend Farmers' Market, mixes in several different bright-flavored herbs, but notes that any or all of them may be omitted and you'll still have a wonderfully tasty salad.

1½ teaspoons mustard seed
1 teaspoon celery seed
3 tablespoons herb vinegar
1½ teaspoons salt
5 cups cooked, sliced, still-warm potatoes
3 hard cooked eggs, chopped
½ - ¾ cup mayonnaise
½ cup finely chopped green onion
1 tablespoon chopped fresh dill weed
1 tablespoon chopped fresh chives
1 tablespoon chopped fresh basil
2 teaspoons chopped fresh tarragon
Freshly ground black pepper to taste
Fresh herb sprigs for garnish

HERB STORAGE: THE LONG AND SHORT TERM OF IT

Cut fresh herb leaves should be rinsed, gently shaken and wrapped lightly in a cotton cloth or bag, then refrigerated. They'll keep longer if you rinse, shake and wrap again every couple of days. If you've purchased whole herb stems, you can stand them up in water and refrigerate them—they'll keep fresh for several days this way.

For longer storage, consider freezing or drying herbs. Both methods are very easy: To freeze, remove stems and flowers, rinse leaves, spin dry in a salad spinner or dry on cloth towels. Place in zip-lock plastic freezer bags and freeze. Simply remove the amount you want just before you need them in a recipe. Frozen herbs are easily chopped, but will darken and wilt as soon as they thaw (their flavor will still be potent, however).

To dry herbs: Gather into a bunch and tie securely around the stems. Rinse and shake to remove dirt and excess moisture, then hang upside down in a dry location. (Wherever this is, it will smell incredibly good for a few days!) Depending upon the weather, the herbs will be dried within 2-4 weeks.

Lay some newspapers on a floor and crumble the dry herbs over the papers. Gather the herbs and crush further, if desired, with your fingers. Fill small clean jars with the dried herbs and label. Store in a cool, dark place. These make excellent gifts, if you can manage to give any up.

DRIED AND TRUE

After you remove the edible herbs from dried bunches, the leftover stems can be also put to good use: tie them together into small bundles—these can be soaked in water and added to hot coals to flavor whatever you are grilling. Add the bundles to a smoldering fire in your fireplace or to a 200-degree oven to make the house smell wonderful. Or use a slender bunch as a basting brush. Herb stems can also perfume a bath to invigorate (sage, rosemary) or calm (marjoram, basil, peppermint) your spirit. In flower arrangements, sachets or potpourri, dried herbs bring the essence of the farm garden to every corner of your home.

1. Combine first four ingredients and, if possible, let stand unrefrigerated for several hours or overnight.
2. Mix all ingredients except garnishes. Refrigerate until ready to serve. Garnish with fresh herb sprigs.

Carol Frank
Allenton, Wisconsin

Herbed New Potatoes, Onions and Peas
4-6 servings

Here's a dish that accents the fresh flavors of three early-summer vegetables with the lively taste of chopped herbs. I like mint, but any of the fresh herbs available at farmers' markets will do the trick. Pick one that will complement your main course . . . dill with grilled fish, cilantro with oriental or hispanic entrees, rosemary with pork or lamb. There's lots of room for variation here. Use early (or spring) onions—the ones with the green stems still on. Select pototoes and onions that are approximately the same size.

½ **pound spring onions OR use small, regular onions (dry-skinned)**
1 pound new red potatoes
⅔ **pound Sugar Snap peas**
1½ tablespoons chopped fresh herbs
Butter or olive oil
Salt and freshly ground black pepper

1. If you're using spring onions, trim off the stems, but leave on a little of the root end and cut an X in the bottom of each, to help them cook evenly and quickly. If you're using onions with dry skins, parboil them 2-3 minutes. Drain. Trim the ends (but leave a little of the root end on) and slip off the skins. Make an X in the root end of each.
2. Scrub potatoes. String the peas. Place potatoes and onions in a pot, cover with water, bring to a low boil and cook until almost tender (about 10-12 minutes, depending upon size). Add peas; boil a few minutes, until all vegetables are tender. Drain. Toss with chopped herbs, butter or oil (you decide the amount), and salt and pepper to taste.

Clams Linguine
with Lots of Fresh Parsley and Garlic
4 servings

This is a quick, familiar pasta dish, full of garlicky goodness and the fresh taste of parsley. It's welcome any time of the year, but seems best for a late summer meal, when tomatoes, garlic and parsley are all fresh from the market. (Fresh clams would be nice, too, but don't count on those in Wisconsin!) If possible, use flat-leaved Italian parsley—it has more flavor than the curly variety. For extra appeal, use spinach linguine. With this dish, a cheerful white wine and good French bread are almost mandatory.

See page 39 for directions on peeling tomatoes.

12 ounces linguine
3 tablespoons olive oil
1 tablespoon minced garlic (or more, if you love garlic)
4 plum tomatoes, peeled and chopped (about 1 cup)
2 cans (each 6½ ounces) chopped clams, drained (reserve juices)
½ cup dry white wine
⅔ cup minced fresh parsley
Freshly ground black pepper
1 cup freshly grated Parmesan cheese

1. Bring a large pot of salted water to boil. Add linguine and boil until barely tender, timing the cooking of the pasta so that it is ready when the sauce is. Have a large, warmed bowl on hand for mixing the pasta with the sauce.
2. While water is heating, warm olive oil and garlic in a large skillet over a low flame 2 minutes.
3. Add chopped tomatoes, ½ cup clam juice and the white wine to pan; simmer 5 minutes.
4. Stir in clams and parsley; heat through. (This will take only a minute or two—don't overdo it or you'll toughen the clams.)
5. Drain pasta, toss in warm bowl with sauce, half the Parmesan and plenty of pepper. Let stand for a moment to allow the pasta to soak up some of the juices, then serve immediately in soup plates (low, flat bowls), with additional Parmesan sprinkled on top.

"Parsley—the jewel of herbs, both in the pot and on the plate."

Albert Stockli,
Swiss chef

"The emotional content of garlic almost equals its culinary value."

Arthur E. Grosser,
author and actor

CHIVE JIVE

The fresh flavor of chives is the easiest thing in the world to save for the colder months when the market is closed. Either buy a potted chive plant to keep indoors or simply chop and freeze cut chives the same day you buy them. Take what you need from the freezer throughout the winter and add the frozen bits directly to your recipes. There's little or no flavor loss.

NUTS TO YOU

To keep nuts fresh—and freshness can make a surprising difference in the taste—store tham airtight in the freezer.

Garlic Chive Dip
Makes 1 ½ cups

Line a wicker basket with a brightly colored cotton towel, then fill it with all manners of trimmed vegetables fresh from the market. Serve with this creamy dip, potent with garlic and chives.

1 cup sour cream, sour half-and-half or plain no-fat yogurt
1 package (3 ounces) cream cheese, softened
1 teaspoon minced garlic
¼ teaspoon salt
⅛ teaspoon black pepper
2 tablespoons chopped fresh or frozen chives

Cream the first two ingredients. Add garlic, salt and pepper; mix until smooth. Stir in chives and refrigerate until ready to serve. Stir once before serving.

Sour Cream or Buttermilk Black Walnut Bread
Makes 1 loaf

Germaine Stank's family recipe for a black walnut quick bread is rich with sour cream and very easy to make. You can substitute low-fat buttermilk for the sour cream and there's virtually no flavor difference. Either way, the distinct, slightly tart goodness of black walnuts comes through. It's real old-fashioned flavor.

1 egg, lightly beaten
1 cup brown sugar
1 cup sour cream or buttermilk
2 cups flour (2¼ cups if using buttermilk)
1 teaspoon baking soda
½ teaspoon baking powder
⅛ teaspoon salt
½ cup chopped black walnuts

1. Preheat oven to 325 degrees. Grease a loaf pan.
2. In a large bowl, mix egg, sugar and sour cream or buttermilk until sugar lumps are gone.
3. Sift flour, baking soda, baking powder and salt. Stir into egg mixture. Fold in nuts.
4. Spread batter in pan; bake 50-55 minutes, until toothpick inserted in center of loaf comes out clean. Cool in pan.

Germaine Stank
Pound, Wisconsin

Hickory Nut Pie
6 servings

Although I no longer go hickory nut picking (see side bar), I still buy the nutmeats at farmers' markets, and I don't blink an eyelash at the price, for I remember long hours with a nut pick. Thank goodness there's still folks like the Pamperins from Juneau willing to spend the time on these treats. Virgelia Pamperin sent her recipe for Hickory Nut Pie; her husband spends his retirement working on his market garden in the summer and cracking hickory nuts in the winter. A noble profession!

1 9-inch, deep-dish unbaked pie crust, store-bought or homemade (see page 16 for recipe)
3 eggs
1 scant cup light corn syrup
4 tablespoons melted butter
½ cup brown sugar
1 tablespoon 100% pure maple syrup or ½ teaspoon maple flavoring
1 heaping cup coarsely chopped hickory nuts
Sweetened whipped cream (see page 70 for method)

1. Preheat oven to 350 degrees. Line a 9-inch deep dish pie pan with homemade crust or thoroughly thaw a frozen, store-bought crust.
2. Beat eggs briefly in a bowl. Add corn syrup and melted butter; beat well until smooth. Stir in brown sugar, maple syrup and nuts; mix thoroughly. Place pie pan on a baking sheet and pour filling into pie shell (if it gets too full, add the last cup after you've put the pan in the oven.) Bake 45-55 minutes, until middle is set. Nuts will have risen to the surface. Cool to room temperature or chill thoroughly. Serve with whipped cream.

Virgelia Pamperin
Juneau, Wisconsin

A HICKORY NUT MEMORY

High on my list of fondest-childhood-memories are the times my older siblings took me hickory nut picking. We would pile into the car on a bright fall weekend, packing peanut butter sandwiches and apples for lunch, and extra paper sacks for collecting the nuts. I don't remember where our particular grove of hickory nut trees was, but it seemed to me it was in another world—a magical one, huge and golden. Cut loose from the car into the crisp air, we'd trample through crunchy leaves in a race to see who could find the most nuts, found fallen at the base of the shaggy-barked nut trees. With luck, I'd locate a motherlode and make an impressive addition to the bushel we filled each year.

Then the real work began, for back home that bushel wasn't nearly as easy to empty as it had been to fill. A hickory nut is a small, pale sphere, and a very hard nut to crack. We used a vise set up in the basement workroom, and filled bowls with cracked nuts that kept idle hands busy for countless hours, picking out the nutmeats.

WISCONSIN'S GOURMET NATIVE

At one time, missionaries called Wisconsin the fabled land of plenty, in reference to the seemingly inexhaustible supply of wild rice that nourished Native Americans. But what was once plentiful is now rare; today, wild rice is known as the caviar of grains.

Gourmet recipes found in many cookbooks have little to do with the way Native Americans prepared wild rice. It was most often boiled and eaten as a porridge or soup. Sometimes it was used as a stuffing or ground into a flour to make bread. At harvest time, a celebration stew of wild rice and game—usually duck—was common. Some kind of animal fat was often mixed into boiled rice, but the typical additions we see today—salt, pepper, butter, chicken stock—are really European influences. More characteristic Native American complements to wild rice include maple syrup, dried or fresh cranberries and blueberries, and bacon drippings. Perhaps the most interesting way native peoples prepared wild rice was to pop it, just like popcorn; popped wild rice was eaten as a cereal or a snack.

Perfect Wild Rice
3-4 servings

You may not be able to afford using wild rice in as many ways as Native Americans did when it was plentiful, but it's a grain well worth your consideration. High in carbohydrates, vitamin B and protein, it's also low in fat and calories. Uncooked wild rice stores almost indefinitely if kept airtight in a cool, dry place, and the cooked grain freezes well.

Genuine wild rice (as opposed to paddy-raised) has long, plump, unbroken grains that cook up tender and chewy, with a rich, nutty flavor. According to Greg Isaksen, who sells wild rice to top chefs around Wisconsin, chicken stock, onions or other flavorings aren't really necessary, just a little salt and pepper.

1 cup genuine wild rice
Salt and freshly ground black pepper
Butter (optional)

Rinse rice well, drain and combine with 3 cups water in a heavy (preferably enameled) pot with a tightly fitting lid. Bring rice to a boil, reduce to a strong simmer (barely boiling), cover and cook 35-45 minutes. Taste it—it should be chewy and just opened up like a hot dog bun, but not overcooked and exploded like popcorn. The rice will not absorb all the water, so drain well when it's done. Season with salt, pepper and, if desired, add a pat of butter.

Greg Isaksen
North Bay Trading Company
Poynette, Wisconsin

Capital Brewery Wild Rice Beer Stuffing
6 side-dish servings or 4 as a main course

I know it's called stuffing, but something that gets as much attention and adoration at holiday meals as the main-dish bird shouldn't be limited to side dish status. Consider serving this hearty Wisconsin combination of wild rice, pork sausage, bread cubes and beer as a brunch or supper main course.

Recipe contributor Richard Lingk recommends using Garten Brau Wild Rice Beer in the stuffing. It's a fitting selection from Capital Brewery of Middleton, Wisconsin.

½ pound bulk pork sausage
1 cup chopped onion
1 cup cooked wild rice (see recipe, page 135)
8 ounces dried bread cubes or unseasoned croutons
½ cup chopped walnuts
¼ teaspoon each dried sage, rosemary, thyme, marjoram and basil
1 bottle (12 ounces) beer
Salt and freshly ground black pepper
1 tablespoon butter, cut into bits (optional)

1. Heat a medium skillet, add sausage and onion and cook until onions are tender.
2. Toss with rice, bread or croutons, walnuts and herbs. Stir in beer; season to taste with salt and pepper.
3. If you're not stuffing a bird, place the mixture in a buttered baking dish and dot it with butter bits. Bake in a glass baking dish at 350 degrees for 35-45 minutes. (Can also be used to stuff one large turkey, 2 chickens or 5-6 game hens.)

Richard Lingk, Board of Directors
Capital Brewery
Middleton, Wisconsin

WILD RICE: HARVESTING HISTORY

There are many good reasons to shop at green markets—economy, nutrition, ecology, enjoyment. The purchases you make at your local farm stands or markets have important cultural significance, too. In Wisconsin, this is never more true than with wild rice. When you buy a package of real wild rice (as opposed to the paddy-raised grain sold at most supermarkets), you're bringing home a taste of Native American tradition and history.

Wild rice is most abundant in Minnesota and northern Wisconsin, where the Chippewa and Winnebago Indian tribes have been harvesting it by hand for centuries. Before European settlers drained wetlands and altered waterways for farmland, wild rice grew all over Wisconsin. To protect the natural fields that now remain, how, when and where wild rice is harvested are strictly regulated today. Laws also protect Native American title rights on reservation waters, as well as their off-reservation gathering rights.

For centuries, wild rice was central to the diets of the Native American tribes who lived where it thrived. In Wisconsin, it provided sustenance to the Chippewa (Ojibway) all year long, but was especially valuable during the lean months. Their belief in wild rice as a spiritual gift is evident by its use in religious ceremonies and celebrations, especially at harvest time. Even now, the wild grass is treated with great reverence by the Chippewa people. Many harvest and process the rice by hand, in much the same way as their ancestors did.

Chef Hacker's Curried Wild Rice Salad
4-6 servings

Here's a tropical treatment for a native Wisconsin grain. See page 135 for instructions on cooking wild rice. To puree pineapple, remove rind and core it, then puree in a food processor or blender.

1 cup plain, no-fat yogurt or mayonnaise
½ cup fresh pineapple puree
1-2 teaspoons curry powder
Salt and freshly ground black pepper
3 cups cooked, cooled wild rice (1 cup raw, see page 135)
¾ cup chopped pecans or hickory nuts
1 stalk celery, finely chopped
½ cup finely chopped bell pepper
½ cup finely chopped green onion
1 cup chopped fresh pineapple
1 cup red seedless grapes, halved
3 oranges—rinds sliced off, cut into segments
1 cup total of any two of the following: raisins, dried cherries, dried cranberries, golden raisins

Whisk yogurt or mayonnaise, pineapple puree and curry powder in a large bowl. Season to taste with salt and pepper. Add remaining ingredients and toss lightly but thoroughly. Serve right away or chill one hour.

Executive Chef Sue Hacker
The Inn at Cedar Crossing
Sturgeon Bay, Wisconsin

Popcorn — Anytime, Any Way

Popcorn is "fresh" very late in the Wisconsin growing season because it must first dry on the stalk, then dry further on the cob after picking. But because of its marvelous keeping power, popcorn is a market purchase that knows no season.

"With or without butter" seems to be the dilemma for cholesterol-conscious popcorn lovers, but there are many ways to enjoy popcorn. Here's some ideas:

Sprinkled with:

Grated Parmesan cheese
Cheddar cheese powder
Hot pepper sauce
Crumbled blue cheese
Brewer's yeast
Sea salt
Garlic salt
No-salt vegetable seasoning
Chili powder
Dill weed

Tossed with:

Maple syrup and toasted nuts
Chow mein noodles and soy sauce
Worcestershire sauce, butter and pretzels
Chocolate chips
Fresh herbs and lemon juice

Made into:

Popcorn balls
Caramel corn (See recipe page 149)
Snack mixes
Popcorn "flour" (ground popped popcorn used in breadings and baked goods)
Breakfast cereal
Brittle candy

Used to make:

Wreaths
Garlands
Ornaments
Environmentally-sound packing material

POPCORN: A REAL KEEPER

Popcorn has been around as a nutritious, fun-to-eat snack for a very long time, possibly as long as 6000 years. Native to the New World, it's inexpensive, popular and available from local growers at Wisconsin farmers' markets.

Airtight, it'll keep on your shelf or in your freezer almost indefinitely. When tiny ears of some 5600-year-old popcorn were found in the Bat Caves of New Mexico, researchers tested the ancient kernels and discovered they still popped.

Legend has it that it was popcorn (and not turkey) that caused the most excitement for colonists at the first Thanksgiving dinner. An Iroquois named Quadequina dumped his popcorn-filled deerskin on the banquet table, and thus introduced the astonished Pilgrims to their first American fun food.

RISING STARS OF THE NORTH:
The Farmers' Markets of Merrill and Ladysmith

Good things come in small packages, and so it is with two fledging farmers' markets in north-central Wisconsin. The towns of Merrill and Ladysmith are fairly small and relatively new at this, but they are both seeing success in the first years of their markets.

August—and the local farmers' market—are going full steam ahead early one Saturday afternoon in Merrill. There's a friendly, community feeling in the air. Maybe it's the sunny weather, but it also has something to do with the two women who take a break from selling to talk about their market. Pat Cadwallader and Helene Pagoria are hardworking growers and lively supporters of the market they helped open in 1990.

The Merrill Area Farmers' Market got started when a volunteer steering committee—given a push by the Lincoln County Extension office and strongly supported by the Chamber of Commerce—formed to develop the concept and set the rules. Pat and Helene agreed to oversee the market's operations for its first two years.

The women are proud of, and excited about, their local market, which takes place in the parking lot that's adjacent to the Sheriff's Department in downtown Merrill. "At first we had pretty wide boundaries, but now only Lincoln County residents can sell here," notes Pat. "They must grow it themselves, too." Both she and Helene are disapproving of markets that allow "buy-and-sell" produce. "That's not a true farmers' market," says Helene. Pat adds: "Our main purpose is to give the little guys a chance. We're not here to sell bananas from wherever."

Quality, honesty and cooperation are emphasized in their market brochure, and that's just what you get from the farmers at the Merrill market. There's a good deal of cleverness, too. One man offers "pet straw" in the fall months, a marketing technique that draws chuckles from passersby. Pat sells "locally-produced" sheep manure and compost. Helene's potted flowers may not be big sellers in August, but "they attract the drivers going by," says Helene. "Once you get them over here, they find something they want."

Ladysmith lies about 60 miles northwest of Merrill. The seasons have changed now and it's a chilling-wet October day to talk with Eric Hillan, who is president of the Rusk County Farm Bureau and was the Ladysmith market's first coordinator. A bald eagle soars high above the market stands while Eric huddles with some of the market regulars in the cold. Usually there's 20 or 30 vendors; today there's only the diehards, the ones who stay "until the snow comes, or the produce is gone!" (This from one of the diehards himself.)

Like his colleagues in Merrill, Eric Hillan sees the new market as a means to support farmers. He's enthusiastic about the environmental and social benefits of markets, but it's clear he's in it first for the local growers.

"The vendors must be from Rusk county, or very close," says Eric. During the first year, Ladysmith's market was sponsored by the Farm Bureau and the County Extension service, but the goal was to put the farmers themselves in the driver's seat. "The vendors should make the decisions," notes Eric. "When a product is in question, they're the ones to decide. One of the farmers, Jim Kurz, is the manager now."

"The market is very popular," says Eric, so popular that the city bought some land downtown and moved the market there from its first location on the Pamida parking lot. "We want it to grow," he adds, and growing it is. It's open two days a week now and crafts are allowed one Saturday per month. That brings more people in, and like the folks in Merrill, Eric and his colleagues know that what's good for the buyer is good for the farmer.

Eric Hillan differs with Helene Pagoria on one point, however. As far as prices go, he says, "They've got to be high enough or we won't survive. Growers have to get enough out of it." According to Helene, "Low is the way to go. The people you're selling to are the people you live with."

What they do agree on, along with Pat Cadwallader, is that it's hard work, farming. ("We don't need prisons; just make 'em pick corn!" laughs Helene.) No matter what the prices are, there just isn't a lot of money in farming. You've got to be in it for more than the dollar. Thank goodness that some folks—like Eric, Helene and Pat—are.

Fresh Market
W·I·S·C·O·N·S·I·N

MAPLE SYRUP,
HONEY AND SORGHUM

Maple Baked Beans
Serves one big crowd (16 or more servings)

Laura Bartz's Maple Baked Beans are rich, smoky-sweet and very addictive. Her recipe makes a lot, but if it's too much for you, halve it or freeze the extras.

2 pounds white or navy beans
½ pound bacon, cut into 1-inch pieces
1 cup catsup
1½ - 2 cups dark maple syrup
1 small onion, chopped
1 tablespoon salt
¼ teaspoon ground black pepper
1 teaspoon dry mustard

1. Sort, wash and soak beans eight hours or longer in cold water. Drain and rinse.
2. Place beans in large, heavy pot, cover with cold water, bring to simmer and cook ½ hour or until a little soft.
3. Meanwhile, cook bacon pieces until crispy. Preheat oven to 350 degrees. Stir bacon, bacon fat and remaining ingredients into the beans. If necessary, add enough hot water to barely cover the beans.
4. Cover pot and bake 2-4 hours until fully tender, stirring once or twice during the first hour. As beans cook, add additional hot water only if necessary. Or, if there's too much liquid, leave the lid off towards the end of cooking. Cooked beans may also be held in a slow oven for several hours. They taste best on the second or third day you serve them. Leftover beans may also be frozen.

Laura Bartz
Suring, Wisconsin

ONE HUNDRED PERCENT WISCONSIN

Those who don't know any better think of Wisconsin as only a farming state, but they've never been to northern Wisconsin. Thousands of small lakes dot the forested landscapes. Rushing rivers create a paradise for fishing enthusiasts. Besides many state and county parks, two gigantic national forests (the Chequamegon and the Nicolet) stretch across the top of the state.

This is maple syrup country. Farmers' markets are few and far between, but motorists don't need to travel far to locate a homestead that sells the sweetest flavor of Wisconsin—maple syrup. Once you try it, you won't ever call the corn-syrupy store-bought versions maple syrup again.

MORE THAN A PANCAKE SYRUP

Maple syrup is available at many markets throughout the state, but some buyers think of it only when pancakes or waffles are on the menu. Yes, it's expensive, but a little goes a long way and it's 100% pure Wisconsin flavor. Combined with local nutmeats like hickory nuts or black walnuts, maple syrup makes an outstanding topping for ice cream, frozen yogurt or frozen custard. Drizzle it on oatmeal, cake slices or muffins; or toss a little with fresh fruit. Replace sugar with maple syrup in a hot bacon dressing, combine with yogurt for a fruit dip— and oh yes, don't forget those pancakes and waffles!

Mom's Granola
6-10 servings

Joel Afdahl, who sent this recipe, operates Uncle Joel's Pure Maple Syrup in Hammond. It started as a hobby over eleven years ago; now the original coffee can buckets and open air cooking have been replaced with networks of plastic tubing that deliver the sap to a cookhouse. No preservatives are used in any of the processing and it takes roughly 40 gallons of sap to make one gallon of syrup. Joel sells his syrup at farmers' markets and grocery stores, and through a mail order business.

Maple syrup and dried cranberries give Joel's granola gourmet status. Use the smaller amount of oil if you're watching the fat.

2½ **cups rolled oats (quick-cooking)**
1 **cup coconut flakes**
½ **cup wheat germ**
½ **cup chopped almonds**
¼ **cup sunflower seeds**
¼ **cup sesame seeds**
¼ **teaspoon salt**
2-4 **tablespoons oil**
½ **cup pure maple syrup**
½ **teaspoon vanilla**
½-¾ **cup dried cranberries or dried cherries (optional)**

Preheat oven to 225 degrees. Combine all ingredients except dried fruit. Spread on an ungreased baking sheet and bake 1-1½ hours, tossing every 20 minutes, until lightly browned. Or, if you prefer granola to stick together somewhat, toss only once during the baking process. Cool and, if desired, add dried fruit. Store tightly covered.

Joel Afdahl
Uncle Joel's Pure Maple Syrup
Hammond, Wisconsin

Maple Dream Bars
Makes 20-25 small bars

Maple Dream Bars are crumbly, cake-like bars that make a fine after-school or coffee-break snack. These maple-y treats taste even better—and the crust is less crumbly—on the second day.

Crust:

1 cup whole wheat or all-purpose white flour
⅛ teaspoon salt
8 tablespoons (1 stick) cold butter, cut into small pieces
1 heaping tablespoon honey

Other Ingredients:

⅔ cup pure maple syrup
3 tablespoons butter
¼ teaspoon salt
2 eggs
½ teaspoon vanilla
1 cup coconut flakes
½ cup chopped walnuts (or other nuts)
2 tablespoons flour
½ teaspoon baking powder

1. To make crust: Preheat oven to 350 degrees. Mix flour and salt, then cut in butter until mixture is texture of cornmeal (may use food processor). Mix in the honey thoroughly. (If using food processor, leave machine on as you add the honey, but turn it off as soon as all the honey is incorporated.) Press dough into an 8-inch square baking dish. Bake 8 minutes.
2. To make bars: Boil maple syrup, butter and salt in saucepan until slightly thickened, about 3-5 minutes. Remove from heat. Beat eggs lightly with vanilla, then whisk into syrup mixture. Combine remaining ingredients and whisk into mixture. Pour over crust and bake until set, about 20 minutes. Cool.

Joel Afdahl
Uncle Joel's Pure Maple Syrup
Hammond, Wisconsin

TIPS
TO TRIM THE FAT
IN YOUR LIFE

• Reduce fat by one-quarter to one-third in quick breads, muffins and cookies.

• In casseroles and main dishes, cut back or eliminate added fat.

• Sauté or stir-fry with very small amounts of fat or use broth or wine instead.

• Chill soups, gravies and stews and skim off the solidified fat before reheating.

• Choose lean meats and trim the fat. Remove skin from chicken.

• Replace sour cream and mayonnaise with non-fat yogurt, buttermilk or pureed cottage cheese. Substitute two egg whites for single eggs. Replace butter with margarine, olive oil or vegetable oil.

From "Revitalize Your Recipes for Better Health," by Christina Stark, M.S., R.D., Division of Nutritional Sciences, Cornell University.

PUMPKIN PUREE

To prepare pumpkin puree from scratch, first get a "pie pumpkin," the kind bred for flavor and not size. They're usually smaller and darker than Halloween pumpkins—just ask the farm stand vendor if you're not sure.

Bake the pumpkin just like you would a potato—poke it with a fork in a few places and bake in a 350-degree oven until tender (a small pumpkin will take about 1½ hours). Slice it open, let it cool somewhat, and remove the seeds (these can be rinsed and toasted with a little salt for a snack). The pumpkin meat can now be easily scooped from the shell and pureed with beaters or a food processor. Once cooled, it freezes beautifully.

Pumpkin Maple Mousse
4-6 servings

Lighter and much easier than pumpkin pie (though believe me, I'm not knocking pumpkin pie!), this Pumpkin Maple Mousse makes a lovely finish to a fall meal. Use only 100% pure maple syrup—from Wisconsin, of course.

If you're using fresh pumpkin puree, be sure the it's at room temperature or chilled before proceeding with the recipe.

1 can (16 ounces) pumpkin OR 1¾ cups cooked, pureed pumpkin (see side bar)
4 tablespoons maple syrup
2 teaspoons finely ground coffee (may also use instant coffee)
½ teapoon ground cinnamon
¼ teaspoon ground cloves
½ cup heavy whipping cream
3 tablespoons sugar
½ teaspoon vanilla
Cinnamon sugar (for garnish)

1. Chill a small, deep bowl and beaters. Meanwhile, in a medium bowl, combine pumpkin, maple syrup, coffee, cinnamon and cloves.
2. In the chilled bowl, whip cream until soft peaks begin to form. Add sugar and vanilla and continue to beat until stiff peaks form.
3. Gently fold whipped cream into pumpkin mixture. Divide into dessert glasses or cups. Chill at least one hour. Sprinkle with cinnamon sugar just before serving.

Maple Nut Sauce for Ice Cream
Makes about 1 cup

½ cup chopped black walnuts, hickory nuts, walnuts or pecans
1 cup pure maple syrup

Toast nuts 5-7 minutes in a preheated 350-degree oven. Meanwhile, boil maple syrup gently, uncovered, in a heavy saucepan until reduced to about ¾ cup. Stir in nuts and cool a little. Serve warm on ice cream or frozen yogurt.

Honey Carrot Cake with Honey Cream Frosting
12-16 servings

Who needs another recipe for carrot cake? If it's this one, we do! Honey lends its distinctive sweetness to an old standby.

Joan Metz of Metz Honey Farm, a blue ribbon winner in honey contests, blends her nectars from clover, locust and basswood trees, and flowers like the Spanish needle wildflower. It's wonderful as is on cereal or muffins or even in coffee or tea, but don't miss the chance to try it (or any of the other honey varieties available at markets) in this special carrot cake.

Cake:

3 eggs
¾ cup honey
¾ cup brown sugar
1 cup vegetable oil
2 cups grated carrots (about ½ pound)
1 can (20 ounces) crushed pineapple, well drained
½ cup raisins
½ cup chopped walnuts (or other nuts)
½ cup coconut flakes
1 teaspoon vanilla
2½ cups flour
2 teaspoons baking soda
2 teaspoons cinnamon
1 teaspoon salt
8 ounces light sour cream OR 1 can (7½ ounces) imitation sour cream

Frosting:

4 tablespoons softened butter or margarine
1 package (8 ounces) cream cheese, softened
½ cup powdered sugar
6 tablespoons honey
Pinch of salt

1. To make cake: Preheat oven to 350 degrees. Grease a 9 by 13-inch baking pan. Beat eggs 15-20 seconds with electric beaters in a large bowl. Mix in honey, brown sugar and oil. Stir in carrots, pineapple, raisins, nuts, coconut and vanilla. Combine flour, baking soda,

SCENES FROM THE MARKET:
Manitowoc

Lake Michigan broods across the street from the Manitowoc Farmers' Market on a stormy day. But it hasn't kept the farmers away . . . or the customers, either:

• Multi-colored umbrellas and billowing raincoats brighten up the drizzle along the double row of produce stands. Vendors try to keep the water off their wares and themselves—clear plastic bags cover human heads and cabbage heads. Coffee steams from a thermos shared by three. A man shrugs when his paper sack soaks through and breaks open, carrots spilling out. "Trying to get away," he chuckles.

• The rain worsens for a few minutes. One brave (and foolish?) woman shops on. "These peppers are beautiful. Really beautiful. There's so many kinds!" she exclaims, standing near a dripping, apparently deserted stand. She chatters on, seemingly to herself, then asks: "How hot are these little red ones?" "Deadly" is the curt, muffled answer that comes from inside the nearby truck. No further help is offered. "I'll take . . . . one," says the subdued woman. An arm reaches out of the truck to take her dime.

Cookbook author Perla Meyers, reminiscing about the Barcelona market in "From Market to Kitchen Cookbook":

"Looking back on my childhood, I consider myself lucky, for it was in this environment, surrounded by these respectful attitudes towards food, that I was taught to appreciate the simplest fare . . . It all contributed to my food education. The simple way of life exposed me to nearly every aspect of food, its cultivation and preparation, and gave me a natural awareness and curiosity when it came to buying and preparing all kinds of ingredients and concoctions. Marketing was woven into the pattern of my life at an early age, and to this day, I continue to explore every market, wherever I may go."

cinnamon and salt; stir into first mixture. Stir in sour cream. Pour into pan; bake 50-60 minutes or until toothpick inserted in center of cake comes out clean. Cool completely before frosting.

2. To make frosting: Beat together all ingredients until smooth. Frost cake and serve chilled or at room temperature.

Joan Metz
Metz Honey Farm
Hazel Green, Wisconsin

Honey Onion Salad Dressing
Makes about 1 cup

Excellent on young and tender spinach leaves. Or, if you've got a bunch of full grown spinach, heat the dressing and "wilt" the salad. This would also make a great sauce for green beans or Brussels sprouts, cold or hot.

2 tablespoons honey
3 tablespoons balsamic or cider vinegar
3 tablespoons finely minced onion
2 tablespoons catsup (optional)
1 teaspoon Worcestershire sauce
⅛ teaspoon salt
⅛ teaspoon black pepper
2 dashes hot pepper sauce
⅓ cup canola oil

Mix all ingredients except oil. Gradually whisk in the oil in a very thin stream. Continue whisking another minute.

Honey Luck Lentils
8-12 servings

These easy baked lentils have the oriental flavorings of soy sauce, orange, ginger and sesame oil, and are smoky-sweet with Wisconsin honey and bacon. I like the way the Chinese give curious names to their dishes—moon cakes, eight-jewel duck, flower rolls—and these lentils are great for a potluck—so this dish was named Honey Luck Lentils.

Be sure to use the dark sesame oil that's used as a flavoring, not the lighter kind that is a cooking or salad oil. This recipe makes a potful of lentils; leftovers freeze well.

4 slices bacon, chopped
1 cup chopped onion
1 teaspoon minced garlic
1 pound lentils
1 cup orange juice
½ cup soy sauce
½ cup honey
2 tablespoons Dijon-style mustard
1 tablespoon dark sesame oil
2 teaspoons grated fresh ginger root
½ teaspoon freshly ground black pepper
½ cup chopped green onions
Hot white rice (optional)

1. Preheat oven to 350 degrees. Heat a heavy, oven-proof pot on top of the stove. Add bacon, cook until half done, then add onion and cook until onion is wilted. Stir in garlic and cook 1 minute longer.
2. Add lentils and 2 cups water, then stir in all but the last two ingredients. Bring to a simmer, cover and place in preheated oven. Bake 60-75 minutes, until liquid is absorbed and lentils are tender. (Can add more water if necessary as the lentils bake.)
3. Sprinkle with chopped green onion and serve alone or with white rice.

IT'S ALL IN THE DISPLAY

Grower Amy Van Ooyen, from the Iron County Farmers' Market, on the allure of an attractive stand:

"This market experience was new for me. I set up a table with a neat golden yellow tablecloth to match my beautiful honey, and displayed my produce. Looking over to my neighbor's stand, I became horrified. Her table was a beautiful arrangement of bright red beets, washed, and the ' tails' on the ends were clipped; orange carrots shiny and clean in neat bunches; Swiss chard so big and fresh you'd love to bite it raw."

"When I looked at my 'hairy' carrots, it was as if I had forgotten to shave my legs, and the tails of my beets drooped sloppily. That first day was a disaster, but it took one week to learn."

Amy learned that even *she* was part of the attraction: *"One Saturday, a young mother approached me and said 'I would like to eat what you grow; you're an advertisement for your own produce.'"*

BASICS IN BRIEF: TOASTED NUTS AND SEEDS

Toasting nuts and seeds brings out all their flavor. To toast nuts, bake at 350 degrees in a single layer 10-15 minutes, tossing once or twice. Watch closely, as they can quickly burn. Sesame, cumin and other seeds can be toasted in a cast iron pan directly over a flame. Toss over medium heat until the seeds are lightly brown and their aroma is released.

Honey Almond Caramel Corn
Makes 2½ quarts

Don't save this one for the holidays—try it now. But watch out, it's a little addictive.

Oil
10 cups popped popcorn
¼ cup dried coconut (optional)
1 cup brown sugar
½ cup honey
2 tablespoons butter
1 tablespoon cider vinegar
½ teaspoon salt
1 cup toasted whole almonds (see side bar), coarsely chopped
½ teaspoon baking soda

1. Oil a very large bowl and a baking sheet. Place popcorn in bowl; sprinkle coconut over it (optional).
2. Pour ½ cup water in a heavy, medium saucepan. Add brown sugar, honey, butter, vinegar and salt. Bring to a boil over medium-high heat and cook until mixture reaches 250 degrees on a candy thermometer.
3. Stir in nuts and continue to cook until mixture reaches 265 degrees. Turn off heat; stir in baking soda (mixture will turn opaque and creamy). Immediately pour over popcorn and stir to coat all the kernels.
4. Spread caramel corn on baking sheet. Cool completely. Break into serving pieces. Store airtight. (A clean-up hint: very hot or boiling water will melt away any sticky mess.)

Hot Honey Lemonade
Makes 4 cups

4 cups lemonade (from frozen concentrate)
3 tablespoons honey
Juice of one lemon
Juice of one orange
6-8 whole cloves
1 large cinnamon stick
4 lemon slices (for garnish)

Combine ingredients and simmer several minutes.

Rainy Day Sorghum Cookies
Makes 3-4 dozen cookies

For a rainy day project, bring out the cookie cutters and make a batch of spicy-sweet sorghum goodies. The dough is lovely to roll out—nice and soft, not sticky or stiff. Umbrella- and boot-shapes would be apropos . . . or how about stars and moons . . . or animal shapes? Spread them with a powdered sugar frosting, if you'd like (see page 85).

The following recipe is from Carol Greipentrog of Dalton, Wisconsin. She and her husband Paul own Turtle Enterprises and sell vegetables, organic chickens and sorghum at Madison's farmers' market.

¼ cup (4 tablespoons) butter
½ cup all-vegetable shortening
1 cup sugar
2 eggs
1 cup sorghum
4 cups flour
1 teaspoon baking soda
1 teaspoon cinnamon
1 teaspoon ground ginger
¼ teaspoon salt
Cinnamon sugar OR powdered sugar frosting (see page 85 for recipe)

1. Cream butter and shortening in a large bowl. Stir in sugar, then beat in eggs. Stir in sorghum and beat until well combined.
2. Combine remaining ingredients (except cinnamon sugar or frosting); stir into first mixture. Dough will be soft. Chill thoroughly.
3. To bake: Preheat oven to 350 degrees. Grease cookie sheets. Roll out the dough ¼ inch thick on a floured surface. Cut shapes with cookie cutters and place carefully on baking sheets at least one inch apart. Sprinkle with cinnamon sugar and bake 12 minutes or until very lightly browned. (Alternately, you may bake the cookies without cinnamon sugar and frost them later.) Gently transfer cookies to wire racks and cool.

Carol and Paul Greipentrog
Turtle Enterprises
Dalton, Wisconsin

SWEET AS SORGHUM

Sorghum is a grain that was first cultivated in Africa around 4000 B.C. and is still widely consumed there and in Asia in the form of bread, cereal and beer. In 19th century America, sorghum was used as a sweetener, along with honey and maple syrup and later, refined sugar beets. Today, our sweet tooth is satisfied mostly by the more convenient cane sugar, but the old-time flavors are still available from many markets and road-side stands.

Sorghum (or more accurately, sorghum syrup) looks and tastes very much like molasses, though it is thinner and lighter, with a fleeting tartness. A little goes a long way.

IT'S A MATTER OF CHOICE
A Taste of Madison

If it's true that variety is the spice of life, then life in Madison, Wisconsin is at its hot-and-spiciest on Dane County Farmers' Market days.

Looking for vegetables? There's baby bok choy, organic onions, fiddlehead ferns, tiny tomatillos and morel mushrooms. There's green peppers, red peppers, yellow peppers, purple peppers. Red tomatoes, orange tomatoes, sun-dried tomatoes, cherry or plum tomatoes. Kohlrabi, Brussels sprouts, leeks, okra. In squashes, you'll find acorn, butternut, spaghetti, patty pans, crooknecks, gourds. Beets, beans, broccoli. Cucumbers, cauliflower, carrots. Greens and garlic. Peas and potatoes. But that's not all.

What about fruits? On the sweet side there's strawberries, blueberries, blackberries, raspberries. Going for tart? Try cranberries, rhubarb, cherries or grapes. There's melons in red, yellow, green and orange. Apples too numerous to name. Pears and plums. Jams and jellies and juices. But that's not all, either.

Cheeses next. Goat or cow? Sharp or mild? Straight or spiked with peppers, chives, veggies or bacon? Cheddar at every age and stage. Smoked cheese, string cheese, cheese curds, cheesecake. Swiss, brick, jack. Mozzarella. Parmesan. Chèvre.

But this is just the beginning! And you're hungry for meat. Chickens, ducks, quails and pheasants. Turkey, partridge, lamb and ham. Liver sausage, summer sausage, Italian sausage, buffalo sausage. Salami, salami, bologna. Kielbasa and knockwurst. Pork chops, spareribs, bacon and brats. And that's not all!

Too tired to cook? Help yourself to onion rolls, sweet rolls, filled croissants. Empanadas and eclairs. Apples dipped in caramel, stuffed in turnovers, fried in fritters. Middle Eastern flatbread. French bread. Nut bread. Fresh pasta, smoked fish.

Then there's chocolate: truffles, brownies, candies, cakes. Chocolate fudge, chocolate doughnuts. Chocolate-dipped fruits and nuts. Chocolate bars and chocolate cows. Not all yet!

The list goes on. Popcorn, and butter to melt over it. Large eggs, mini-eggs, brown eggs, green eggs. Herb vinegars, garlic braids, pestos. Fresh flowers, dried flowers, potted flowers, bouquets.

Maple syrup, sorghum, honey. Plants to hang and plants to plant. Houseplants, hickory nuts, herbs galore.

Eggplants that look like eggs. Pumpkins the size of furniture. Onions you eat like apples.

Mountains made of beans.

Mountains made of corn.

And that's not all!

Fresh Market
W·I·S·C·O·N·S·I·N

APPENDICES AND INDEX

THE FARMERS' MARKETS OF WISCONSIN

Wondering if there's a fresh food market near your home? Looking for some local flavor while traveling the state? Or maybe you're a producer in search of customers. This list of Wisconsin's farmers' markets was first developed as part of a direct marketing research project sponsored by the University of Wisconsin-Platteville and the University of Wisconsin-Extension.

Market schedules and locations are subject to change. While not all Wisconsin markets are operated by local chambers of commerce or county extension offices, those offices may be contacted for up-to-date information about newly established markets, changes in existing farmers' markets and who to contact about becoming a vendor. See page 159 for a map.

1. **Algoma Municipal Farmers' Market**
   American Legion Grounds
   Saturdays, June-October
   7:00 am - Sold

2. **Appleton Farm & Fleet Market**
   Goodwill Parking Lot
   Highway 47
   4th Saturdays, April-August;
   All Saturdays, September-October
   7:00 am - Sold

3. **Ashland Municipal Farmers' Market**
   Coast to Coast Parking Lot
   U.S. Highway 2 and Front Street
   Saturdays, mid-August - early October
   8:00 am - noon

4. **Beaver Dam Mall Farmers' Market**
   Beaver Dam Mall
   Wednesdays and Saturdays,
   June-October
   7:00 am - Sold

5. **Beloit Farmers' Market**
   300 Block of State Street (Downtown)
   Saturdays, June-October
   8:00 am - 1:00 pm

6. **Black River Falls -**
      Municipal Farmers' Market
   City Hall Parking Lot
   101 S. Second Street
   Monday-Saturdays, June-November
   Hours vary

7. **Cambridge Municipal Farmers' Market**
   Village Square Park
   Last Tuesdays, April-November
   7:00 am - noon

8. **Chippewa Falls Farmers' Market**
   Downtown
   Thursdays, late June-October
   3:00 pm - Dark

9. **Clintonville Municipal Farmers' Market**
   Downtown Bridge Parking Lot
   Saturdays, August-October
   8:00 am - Sold

10. **Columbus Farmers' Market**
    Dickason Blvd.
    First Tuesdays, May-October
    6:00 am - noon

11. **Crandon Municipal Farmers' Market**
    Highway 8 East
    Saturdays, June-October
    8:00 am - 1:00 pm

12. **DePere - East DePere Farm Market**
    Marquette Mall
    Thursdays, July-October
    7:00 am - noon

13. **DePere -**
       Municipal Farmers' Market - West
    Nicolet Square
    Tuesdays, July-October
    7:00 am - noon

14. **Dodgeville -**
    Municipal Farmers' Market
    City Parking Lot
    Saturdays, June-November
    7:00 am - Sold

15. **Eau Claire -**
    Municipal Farmers' Market
    Downtown Parking Lot
    East Lake and South Farwell Streets
    Wednesdays and Saturdays,
      June-October
    8:00 am - Sold

16. **Elkhart Lake Farmers' Market**
    Elkhart Lake Depot
    Saturdays, July-September
    8:30 am - noon

17. **Fennimore Municipal Farmers' Market**
    Tuckwood House
    1280 10th Street
    Saturdays, June-November
    8:00 am - Sold

18. **Fond du Lac Municipal Farmers' Market**
    Parking Lot #8, Portland Street
    Saturdays, June-October
    6:00 am - 2:00 pm

19. **Frederic Farmers' Market**
    Inter-County Cooperative Publishing
      Parking Lot
    Saturdays, mid-July - September
    8:00 am - noon

20. **Green Bay Municipal Farmers' Markets**
    Cherry and Quincy Streets
    Saturdays, July-November
    7:00 am - noon

    Military Avenue and Mason Street
    Wednesdays, July-November
    7:00 am - noon

21. **Hartford Municipal Farmers' Market**
    Old City Garage
    Saturdays, May-November
    7:00 am - noon

22. **Hartland Farmers' Market**
    North Avenue, across from Valley Bank
    Saturdays, July-October
    9:00 am - noon

23. **Horicon Municipal Farmers' Market**
    Marshland Mart
    Highway 33 west of Horicon
    Thursdays, May-November
    7:00 am - Sold

24. **Hudson Municipal Farmers' Market**
    Mid-America Bank Parking Lot
    2nd and Vine Streets
    Thursdays, May-Frost
    8:00 am - Sold

25. **Hurley - Iron County Farmers' Market**
    Business Highway 51 and 10th Avenue
    Saturdays and Wednesdays,
      July 15 - October 15
    Saturdays: 10:00 am - Sold;
    Wednesdays: 2:00 pm - Sold

26. **Janesville Municipal Farmers' Market**
    Rock River Plaza
    South River and South Main Streets
    Saturdays, June-October
    8:00 am - 2:00 pm

27. **Jefferson Municipal Farmers' Market**
    Behind City Hall
    3rd Tuesdays, May-November
    6:00 am - Sold

28. **Kenosha Municipal Farmers' Markets**
    June-November
    Mondays: Roosevelt Park,
      34th Avenue and Roosevelt Road;
      and Anderson Park,
      87th Place and 26th Avenue
    Tuesdays: Union Park,
      45th Street at 8th Avenue
    Wednesdays and Saturdays:
      Columbus Park,
      54th Street at 22nd Avenue
    Thursdays: Lincoln Park,
      18th Avenue and 70th Street
    Fridays: Baker Park,
      66th Street and Sheridan Road
    6:00 am - noon
    (until 1:00 pm on Saturdays)

29. **La Crosse Farmers' Market**
City Hall Parking Lot
4th and La Crosse Streets
Saturdays, June-October
6:00 am - Sold

30. **La Crosse Farmers' Market**
Bridgeview Plaza
2400 Rose Street
Wednesdays, June-October
6:00 pm - Sold

31. **Ladysmith Farmers' Market**
Downtown on Highway 8
Saturdays, June-October
9:00 am - 1:00 pm

32. **Lake Mills Municipal Farmers' Market**
Lake Mills City Park
2nd Saturdays, June-October
6:00 am - Sold

33. **Lancaster Municipal Farmers' Market**
Courthouse Parking Lot
Saturdays, June-October
7:00 am - noon

34. **Madison -**
Dane County Farmers' Markets
Capitol Square
Saturdays, last Saturday in April-
first Saturday in November
6:00 am - 2:00 pm

Martin Luther King Jr. Blvd.
Wednesdays, May-October
9:30 am - 2:00 pm

35. **Madison - Hilldale Farmers' Market**
Hilldale Mall Parking Lot
Wednesdays and Saturdays,
early May-October
7:00 am - 2:00 pm

36. **Madison - High Point Center**
Behind WestTowne Mall
Wednesdays and Saturdays,
June-October
Wednesday: 3:00 pm - Dark;
Saturday: 8:00 am - 2:00 pm

37. **Manitowoc Municipal Farmers' Market**
Lakeview Center, 828 Memorial Drive;
and Edgewater Plaza, Magnolia Drive
Tuesdays & Saturdays, May 1-November
6:00 am - Sold

38. **Marinette Municipal Farmers' Market**
Stephenson Street,
behind Lauerman Building
Tuesdays & Fridays, July-October
7:30 am - noon

39. **Mayville Municipal Farmers' Market**
Main Street
Wednesdays, June-October
7:00 am - 1:00 pm

40. **Medford -**
Taylor County Farmers' Market
Taylor Country Fairgrounds
Highways 13 & 64
Saturdays, July-October
8:30 am - 1:00 pm

41. **Menomonie Farmers' Market**
Corner of 2nd and Main Streets
Saturdays, mid-July - October
7:00 am - 2:00 pm

42. **Merrill Area Farmers' Market**
Wednesdays: Pamida Parking Lot,
Highway 64
Saturdays: Northwest Corner of
Business Highways 51 & 64
June 15-October 30
7:00 am - 2:00 pm or Sold

43. **Middleton Farmers' Market**
Middleton Springs Shopping Center
2500 Allen Blvd.
Saturdays and Thursdays,
last Sat. in May-October
Saturday: 8:00 am - Sold;
Thursday: 1:00 pm - Sold

44. **Milton Community Market Days**
Railroad Park, Milton Junction
First Saturdays, May-September
8:00 am - 1:00 pm

45. **Milwaukee -**
    Municipal Farmers' Markets
    (Green Markets)
    (Locations and times may change -
       call 414-223-5700)
    2200 W. Fond du Lac
    Monday-Saturday, 7:00 am - 7:00 pm

    4th and Wisconsin Avenue (Downtown)
    Wednesdays, 10:00 am - 4:00 pm

    Mitchell at 14th
    Monday-Saturday, 7:00 am - 7:00 pm

46. **Monroe Municipal Farmers' Market**
    Parking Lot Behind Junior High School
    Wednesdays & Saturdays, May-October
    7:00 am - Sold

47. **Neillsville Municipal Farmers' Market**
    Parking Lot on Main and 5th
    Saturdays, May-October
    9:00 am - noon

48. **New Holstein -**
    Municipal Farmers' Market
    Fire Station on Highway 57
    Saturdays, July-November
    8:00 am - noon

49. **New Richmond Farmers' Market**
    New Richmond Heritage Center
    Saturdays, mid-July - October
    8:00 am - 2:00 pm

50. **Oconomowoc Farmers' Market**
    Village Green (Downtown)
    Saturdays, mid-June - October
    7:30 am - noon

51. **Oshkosh Municipal Farmers' Market**
    Riverside Park
    Wednesdays & Saturdays, June-October
    Wednesdays: 1:00 pm - Sold;
    Saturdays: 8:00 am - noon

52. **Platteville Farmers' Market Place**
    Main Street City Parking Lot
    Saturdays, 2nd Sat. in April-
       2nd Sat. in October
    6:00 am - noon

53. **Port Washington Farmers' Market**
    Main and Franklin
    Saturdays, July-October
    8:00 am - noon

54. **Portage Farmers' Markets**
    Northridge Parking Lot
    Fridays, May-November
    7:30 am - 1:00 pm

    Market Square
    Saturdays, May-November
    7:30 am -1:00 pm

55. **Prairie du Chien -**
    Municipal Farmers' Market
    Prairie City Bank Lot
    Saturdays, May - mid-October
    7:00 am - 11:00 am

56. **Princeton Cattle Fair**
    2nd and Main Streets
    First Wednesdays, April-November
    7:00 am - 4:00 pm

57. **Racine Municipal Farmers' Markets**
    Main Street Farmers' Market
    South End of Main Street Bridge
    Saturdays, June-November
    8:00 am - 1:00 pm

    Monument Square Mall Market
    Monument Square East
    Tuesdays & Fridays, June-November
    9:00 am - 2:00 pm

58. **Racine Southside Farmers' Market**
    c/o Grace Mears 414-886-3284
    Mondays, Wednesdays & Fridays,
       June-November
    8:00 am - noon

59. **Racine County - Seven Mile Fair**
    I-94 & Seven Mile Road in Racine County
    Saturdays & Sundays, April-October
    7:00 am - 5:00 pm

60. **Reedsburg Municipal Farmers' Market**
    300 Block of East Main Street
    Daily, May-November
       (vendor attendance varies)
    Hours vary

61. **Rice Lake Municipal Farmers' Market**
    South Main Street
    Open days and hours
       (vendor attendance varies)

62. **Richland Center -**
    Richland Farmers' Market
    Community Center Parking Lot
    Seminary Street
    Wednesdays & Saturdays, June-October
    7:30 am - 11:00 am

63. **Ripon Farmers' Market**
    400 Watson Street
    Tuesdays, Thursdays & Saturdays,
       July-October
    Tuesday & Saturday: 7:00 am - Sold;
    Thursday: 3:30 pm - Sold

64. **River Falls Municipal Farmers' Market**
    West Maple and Clark Streets
    Mondays-Saturdays, June-October
    7:00 am - Sold

65. **Shawano Area Farmers' Market**
    Fairview Plaza on Highway 29
       (East Green Bay Street)
    Saturdays, May-October
    8:00 am - 1:00 pm

66. **Sparta Farmers' Market**
    313 S. Water Street - Downtown
    Wednesdays and Saturdays,
       2nd Saturday in June-October
    Wednesday: 4:00 pm - 7:00 pm;
    Saturday: 8:00 am - noon

67. **Stevens Point Farmers' Market**
    Mathias Mitchell Public Square
    Daily, year-round
    6:00 am - Sold

68. **Stoughton Municipal Farmers' Market**
    Main and Division Streets
    Fridays, last week in May-October
    7:00 am - noon

69. **Sturgeon Bay -**
    Municipal Farmers' Market
    Market Square
    Saturdays, late June-October
    9:00 am - 12:30 pm

70. **Sun Prairie Farmers' Market**
    American Legion Hall Parking Lot
    411 E. Main
    Saturdays, June-October
    8:00 am - Sold

71. **Viroqua Farmers' Market**
    Downtown
    Saturdays, 1st Saturday in May -
       3rd Saturday in October
    7:30 am - 1:00 pm

72. **Watertown Municipal Farmers' Market**
    North 1st Parking Lot
    2nd Tuesdays
    7:00 am - noon

73. **Waukesha Farmers' Market**
    Corner of Main and Barstow, Downtown
    Tuesdays, Thursdays & Saturdays,
       May-November
    7:00 am - 1:00 pm

74. **Waupaca Municipal Farmers' Market**
    Public Square, East Fulton Street
    Daily, May-October
    7:00 am - 7:00 pm

75. **Wausau -**
    Farmers' Market of Wausau, Inc.
    300 River Drive
    Wednesdays and Saturdays,
       June-November
    6:00 am - 6:00 pm

76. **West Allis Farmers' Market**
    1559 S. 65th Street
    Tuesdays, Thursdays & Saturdays,
       May-November
    1:00 - 8:00 pm

77. **West Bend Farmers' Market**
    Main Street, Downtown
    Saturdays, mid-June - October
    7:30 am - 11:00 am

78. **Westfield -**
    Marquette County
    Vegetable Cooperative
    Pioneer Parking Lot
    Daily, May-November
    9:00 am - 6:00 pm

THE FARMERS' MARKETS OF WISCONSIN

3.
Ashland   25.
Hurley

19. Frederic

11. Crandon

61.
Rice Lake
31. Ladysmith

New Richmond
49.

40. Medford   42.
Merrill

Marinette 38.

Hudson
24.

Chippewa Falls
64.   41.   8.
River Falls   Menomonie
15.
Eau Claire

75.
Wausau

65.
Shawano

69.
Sturgeon Bay

Algoma
1.

9. Clintonville

47. Neillsville   Stevens Point
67.

20. Green Bay
12.
13. DePere

6.
Black River Falls

74.
Waupaca   Appleton 2.

Manitowoc
37.

Sparta
66.

Oshkosh 51.

63.
Ripon

48.
New Holstein

29.
30. La Crosse

78. Westfield   18.
56. Princeton   Fond du Lac

16. Elkhart Lake

53.   Port
Washington

Viroqua
71.

Reedsburg
60.   54. Portage

Beaver
Dam 4.

Mayville
39.   West Bend
23. Horicon 77.

Richland Center
62.

Columbus 10.

72.   21. Hartford
Watertown 22. Hartland

55. Prairie du Chein   14. Dodgeville

70. Sun Prairie
34.
35. Madison 32. Lake Mills
Middleton 43.   36.
68.   7. Cambridge 50. Oconomowoc

45. Milwaukee

Stoughton 27. Jefferson
Waukesha 73.

17. Fennimore
33. Lancaster
52. Platteville   Monroe
46.

44. Milton

57. 58. 59. Racine
28. Kenosha

76. West Allis

Janesville 26.

Beloit 5.

WISCONSIN HARVEST CALENDAR

This guide estimates when fruits and vegetables are available at local farmers' markets and roadside stands. The calendar generally reflects the southern half of the state, where the majority of Wisconsin farms—and farm markets—are located.

Remember that many market products like cheese, maple syrup and hydroponically-raised vegetables are available through most or all of the season. In addition, the proper storage of some produce will extend the market season, so don't assume that the end of harvest means an item is no longer available.

□ = Some availability;   ■ = Peak season

"1" following a month indicates the first half of the month,   "2" indicates the second half

	Apr 2	May 1	May 2	Jun 1	Jun 2	Jul 1	Jul 2	Aug 1	Aug 2	Sep 1	Sep 2	Oct 1	Oct 2	Nov 1
Apples								□	□	■	■	■	■	□
Asparagus		□	■	■	□									
Basil							□	■	■	□				
Beans						□	□	■	■	■	□			
Beets					□	□	■	■	■	■	■	□		
Broccoli						□	□	■	■	■	■	□	□	
Brussels Sprouts									□	□	■	■	■	
Cabbage					□	■	■	■	■	■	■	□	□	
Carrots						□	□	■	■	■	■	□	□	□
Cauliflower						□	□	■	■	■	■	□	□	
Cherries						□	■	□	□					
Cilantro		□	■	■	■	□	□			□	□	□	□	
Corn						□	□	■	■	□				
Cranberries										□	■	■	□	
Cucumbers				□	□	■	■	■	□	□	□			
Dill		□	□	□	□	□	□	□	□	□	□	□		
Eggplant							□	■	■	■	□	□		
Greens (Kale, etc.)					□	□	□	■	■	■	□	□	□	
Leeks	□	□							□	■	■	■	■	□
Lettuce			□	■	■	□	□	□	□	□	□	□		
Melons								□	□	■	■	□	□	
Mushrooms	□	□	□	□	□	□	□	□	□	□	□	□	□	
Onions			□	□	□	□	□	□	■	■	■	■	■	□
Parsley			□	□	□	■	■	■	■	■	■	□	□	□
Peas				■	■	□				□	□			
Pears									□	□	■	■	■	□
Peppers							□	■	■	■	■	□		
Potatoes						□	□	□	■	■	■	□	□	□
Pumpkins										□	□	■	■	□
Radishes		□	□	■	■	□	□				□	□	□	
Raspberries							□	■	■	□	□	□	□	
Rhubarb		□	■	■	□	□								
Spinach			□	□	■	■	□	□	□	□	□	□	□	
Squash (Summer)					□	□	■	■	■	■	□	□		
Squash (Winter)									□	□	■	■	■	□
Strawberries				■	■	□								
Tomatoes							□	■	■	■	□	□		
Turnips, Rutabagas								□	□	■	■	■	■	□
Watercress	■	■	■	□	□	□					□	□	□	

IS IT FRESH? IS IT RIPE? HOW TO TELL . . .

APPLES
Look for: Firm, crisp, well-shaped fruit with good color fitting to its variety. There are many apple varieties and their flavors develop from week to week, so it's best to ask the vendor to advise you about maturity. Better yet, taste before you buy. Stem-on apples keep better.
Avoid: Shriveled, soft or bruised apples. Listless color. Mealy texture.

ASPARAGUS
Look for: Rounded, straight stalks with tightly closed, compact tips. Bright green color running as far down the spear as possible (only the green part is edible). Choose evenly sized spears for uniform cooking.
Avoid: Ridged or very dirty spears. Broken or splayed tips. Woody or dry ends. Reedy or extremely thick stalks.

BEANS (SNAP)
Look for: Smooth, firm pods that snap crisply and look moist inside. Lively color, whether green, yellow or purple.
Avoid: Pods that are limp, bulging, pitted, over-thick or fibrous.

BEETS
Look for: Smooth, firm, richly colored beets of small to medium size. Slender roots. Lively-looking tops.
Avoid: Excessively hairy roots. Wilted tops. Brown, scaly areas near the "shoulders" (indicates toughness). Soft or shriveled beets.

BROCCOLI
Look for: Compact, tightly clustered flowerets atop firm stalks. Some drying at the end of the stalk is normal, but the sides should be green and fresh-looking. Bud clusters should have deep color: dark green or purplish-green.
Avoid: Open or flowering buds. Heads that are yellowing. Excessively thick, woody or whitish stems. Open cores at the base of the stalk.

BRUSSELS SPROUTS
Look for: Firm, green, unblemished heads with no signs of yellowing. Tight-fitting leaves.
Avoid: Sprouts that are loose-leaved, black-spotted, puffy or lightweight for their size.

CABBAGE
Look for: Firm, hard, smooth, heavy heads with closely-trimmed stems. Outer leaves should be tight-fitting, blemish-free and deep green or purplish red, depending on the variety. (Savoy cabbage will have curly leaves and more loosely-formed heads.)
Avoid: Heads with an excess of loose or wilted outer leaves. Heads that are lightweight for their size, badly blemished, soft or yellowing.

CARROTS

Look for: Smooth surface and bright color all the way to the "shoulders." Firm texture. Lively-looking, bright green tops.

Avoid: Flabby, shriveled or cracked carrots. Huge size or an excessive amount of stem shoots indicate tough, woody cores.

CAULIFLOWER

Look for: Clean, compact, firm heads with good weight for their size. Color should be bright white or creamy white. If outer leaves are intact, they should be green and fresh.

Avoid: Cauliflower that is bruised, brown-speckled, yellowing, mealy-looking or soft. Don't buy it if the curds (the edible white flowerets) are spreading open.

CHERRIES (TART)

Look for: Plump, firm, smooth cherries with a bright, glassy red color and fresh-looking stems.

Avoid: Cherries with soft, discolored or moldy flesh, or dried-up stems. Overmature cherries look dull or shriveled and feel sticky. Immature fruit is small, hard and pale.

CORN

Look for: Fresh-looking, tight husks of a good green color. Plump, firm kernels that reach to the tip of the cob and offer some resistance to pressure, but squirt a little when pressed firmly or pierced. Color ranging from creamy white to yellow, depending on the variety. The stem end of very fresh corn will look moist and pale green. Corn kept cool retains sweetness longer.

Avoid: Tiny, underdeveloped kernels. Old ears with very large, deep-yellow kernels. Signs of decay or worms. Pale or yellowish, wilted husks. Brownish, dry-looking stem ends. Corn that is warm to the touch.

CRANBERRIES

Look for: Very firm, plump, deep to dark red berries with lustrous, smooth skin. An official test of freshness at sorting stations is to see if the cranberries bounce.

Avoid: Cranberries that are small, extra hard and light in color are immature. Spongy, dull-looking, leaky berries are overmature.

CUCUMBERS

Look for: Firm, smooth green cucumbers of medium size and crisp texture. (Pickling cucumbers should be small and hard with a warted, spiny surface.)

Avoid: Huge, puffy-looking cucumbers. Ones with soft spots, a shriveled look or yellowish color. Very hard cukes are underripe.

EGGPLANT

Look for: Small to medium-size eggplants heavy for their size. A glossy, firm and unblemished surface that yields slightly to pressure, but springs back when released. Smooth skin with a deep purple or creamy white color. The green cap should be bright and unshriveled.

Avoid: Over-sized, pitted or flabby eggplants. A green cast just below the skin or throughout the flesh indicates immaturity.

GREENS (KALE, ETC.)

Look for: Crisp, lively-looking leaves with a tender bite and healthy green color.
Avoid: Greens that are limp or yellowing, have fibrous stems or an excess of insect holes.

HERBS

Look for: Lively-looking, green, unblemished leaves and stems.
Avoid: Wilted or discolored leaves or stems.

LEEKS

Look for: Firm stems with several inches of white on the bulb end, and green, lively-looking tops.
Avoid: Leeks that are oversized, have flabby, yellowing tops or tough, fibrous stems.

LETTUCE

Look for: Fresh and lively-looking leaves with pale to deep green color, depending on the variety. Iceberg (head) lettuce should be firm and compact. Romaine ribs should be crisp and white. Leaf lettuce should be tender.
Avoid: Wilted, pitted or rusted leaves. Avoid iceberg lettuce that lacks green color or is irregularly-shaped.

MELONS

Look for: There are several types, but generally go for firm, symmetrical fruit that's heavy for its size. Ripe fruit will feel a little soft near the stem end when pressed lightly, and will smell faintly of the sweet fruit when sniffed there. Also, a sunken scar located at the stem end means the fruit ripened on—and was easily plucked from—the vine. You'll get the best flavor from these, but slightly immature melons will ripen nicely at home. Ripe canteloupes pierce easily along a seam.
Avoid: A greenish tinge. Very hard or very soft rind. Signs of decay like dark, sunken spots or a strong, heavily sweet odor.

MUSHROOMS

Look for: Cultivated white mushrooms should be firm and plump, have short stems and a creamy white color. The gills should be pinkish or tan. Morels should be springy and heavy for their size. Shiitakes should be firm and have a woody smell.
Avoid: Oversized mushrooms, and ones with opened caps, dark gills or a pitted surface.

ONIONS

Look for: Very firm, well-shaped onions with plenty of dry, crackling skin and no blemishes. Green onions should be deep green along the stem and bright white on the bulb end, crisp and fresh-looking.
Avoid: Soft or sprouted onions. Greenness around the neck, or sootiness. Very dry and woody neck ends indicate over-ripeness. For green onions, avoid wilted or flabby onions and ones that are oversized.

PEARS

Look for: Firm, plump, good-sized pears that are beginning to soften. Color, size and even firmness depend on the variety, and like apples, pear flavor changes as the season progresses, so ask the grower for advice or a taste. Ripe pears bruise very easily, so for safer transportation the fruit is usually picked when it's not quite ripe. Ripened at home, pears are ready to eat when they yield easily to soft pressure.
Avoid: Badly bruised pears, or ones that are very hard or getting mushy.

PEAS

Look for: Crisp, well-filled, firm pods that snap when you bend them. Bright green color.
Avoid: Dry seams or tips. Overmature pods are light for their size and swollen. Flat, darkish peas are immature (except for Snow peas, which should be flat). Avoid peas that are sitting in the sun—warm peas lose their sugar content quickly.

PEPPERS

Look for: Firm, glossy, thick-fleshed, weighty peppers. Whether red, yellow, orange or green, the color should be bright. Deep purple peppers are also available.
Avoid: Peppers that have soft or watery spots, are wilted, thin-skinned or scarred.

POTATOES

Look for: Firm, well-shaped, smooth-skinned potatoes.
Avoid: Potatoes with green cast or spots, bruises or sprouts, leathery skin.

PUMPKINS

See Squash (Winter)

RADISHES

Look for: Firm, smooth, plump, well-shaped radishes of medium size. Deep red or white color. Crisp-looking tops.
Avoid: Oversized radishes, or ones with decayed tops, black spots or dry, hollow interiors.

RASPBERRIES

Look for: Clean, dry-looking, plump berries uniformly colored a deep, vivid red. They should look somewhat velvety. By all means, sample the berries of several vendors to find the the sweetest ones. Perfectly ripe raspberries are fragile—and expensive—so treat them with care.
Avoid: Stained containers, mushiness, leakiness and dull color indicate berries that are past their prime. Too-firm raspberries with the stems attached are immature.

RHUBARB

Look for: Fresh, firm, crisp, glossy stalks of medium thickness. Best flavor comes from deep red or pinkish stalks.
Avoid: Flabby, or excessively thick or thin stalks. Pale green stalks are immature. Do not eat the poisonous leaves.

SPINACH
Look for: Fresh, tender lively-looking leaves of bright green.
Avoid: Wilted, bruised or yellowing spinach. Overdeveloped spinach will be thick, tough and sprouting.

SQUASH (SUMMER)
Look for: Firm, shiny, smooth-skinned squash of small to medium size. Should be relatively heavy for its size and blemish-free. Outside color depends on variety, but inside should be creamy white, and seeds should be small.
Avoid: Squash with hard, tough or dull-looking surface. Soft or brown spots. Oversized squash. Flabbiness or softness.

SQUASH (WINTER)
Look for: Select squash with a hard, tough rind, one that's heavy for its size. No signs of mushiness. Deep color, depending upon variety. Attached stem end.
Avoid: Soft spots. Stemless winter squash won't keep well. Tender skin indicates immaturity.

STRAWBERRIES
Look for: Stem on, medium size berries that are clean, dry, fresh-looking and brightly colored. They should yield to gentle pressure, but shouldn't be over-soft. Ripe fruit has a heady, berry-like aroma. Sweet, ripe strawberries are glorious, but the season is short and many things affect flavor, so taste and compare to get the best berries possible.
Avoid: Greenish or whitish cast. Too many or oversized seeds. Very small or very large berries lack flavor, depending on the variety. Too-firm berries are immature, too-soft ones are overripe. Avoid moldy berries.

TOMATOES
Look for: Firm, smooth-skinned, unblemished tomatoes. Generally size doesn't signal quality, but do choose plump ones. Fully ripe tomatoes will have a deep, rich red (or yellow) color and will give a little when gently pressed. They also have a rich, distinctive, earthy smell. Less mature fruits will be firmer and less intense in color, and are a good choice if the tomatoes are to ripen at home.
Avoid: Cracked, badly blemished or splotchy tomatoes. Very soft tomatoes are overripe. Hard or greenish ones were picked immature and won't develop the full vine-ripened flavor, although they have a culinary appeal of their own. Don't purchase cold tomatoes; once chilled, they lose flavor and good texture.

TURNIPS, RUTABAGAS
Look for: Smooth, firm, rounded vegetables with lively-looking green tops. Medium size. Heavy for their size.
Avoid: Oversized, badly blemished or flabby vegetables. Wilted or discolored tops.

BIBLIOGRAPHY

While this is but a partial listing of the resources used in the writing of this book, the following materials provided inspiration and/or particularly useful information.

Behr, Edward. "The Artful Eater." New York: The Atlantic Monthly Press, 1992.

Carlman, Susan F. "Farmers Market Cookbook." Chicago: Chicago Review Press, Inc., 1988.

Clark, Robert, ed. "Our Sustainable Table...Essays." San Francisco: North Point Press, 1990.

Cottingham, John, et al. "The Direct Marketing Newsletter." Platteville, WI: Cooperative Extension Programs, University of Wisconsin-Extension and University of Wisconsin-Platteville.

Hachten, Harva. "The Flavor of Wisconsin." Madison, WI: The State Historical Society of Wisconsin, 1981.

Eating Well magazine. Charlotte, VT: Eating Well Magazine, Scott Mowbray, ed.

Fannucchi, Genevieve T. and William A., and Scott Craven. "Wild Rice in Wisconsin: Its Ecology and Cultivation." Madison, WI: University of Wisconsin-Extension and Department of Agricultural Journalism, in cooperation with the United States Department of Agriculture.

Fisher, M.F.K. "The Art of Eating." New York: Collier Books-Macmillan Publishing Company, various copyrights from 1937 to 1990.

Killingstad, Helen, et al. "Take Home . . . Something Special from Wisconsin." Wisconsin Department of Agriculture, Trade & Consumer Protection, Marketing Division, July 1989.

Klingbeil, G.C., and J.M. Rawson. "Wisconsin Cranberry Lore." Wisconsin: University of Wisconsin-Extension, in cooperation with the United States Department of Agriculture.

McGee, Harold. "On Food and Cooking." New York: Collier Books-Macmillan Publishing Company, 1984.

McPhee, John. "Giving Good Weight." United States: McGraw-Hill, 1979.

Morash, Marian. "The Victory Garden Cookbook." New York: Alfred A. Knopf, 1982.

Olney, Judith. "The Farm Market Cookbook." New York: Doubleday, 1991.

Rural Enterprises magazine. Menomonee Falls, WI: The Brady Company, Karl F. Ohm III, ed. and pub.

Pyle, Jane. "Farmers' Markets in the United States: Functional Anachronisms." Geographical Review, Vol. LXI, No. 2, April 1971, pp. 167-197.

Sax, Richard, with Sandra Gluck. "From the Farmers' Market." New York: Harper & Row, Publishers, 1986.

Wanderer, Pauli. "Cooking in Door County." Edina, MN: Voyageur Press Inc., 1985.

"Wisconsin Talks" Radio Program. Host Jean Feraca interviews cookbook author Judith Olney about farmers' markets, Wisconsin Public Radio, June 19, 1991.

Wisconsin Trails magazine. Madison, WI: Wisconsin Tales and Trails, Inc., Howard Mead, ed. and pub.

INDEX

For additional copies of this book contact:

AMHERST PRESS

318 N. Main St.

Amherst, WI 54406

or Call: 715-824-3214   or   Tollfree: 1-800-333-8122

FAX orders to: 715-824-5806